Target
Study Skills

○ TARGET READING SKILLS FOR LIFE SERIES

D1515585

AGS
PUBLISHING

Circle Pines, Minnesota 55014-1796
800-328-2560
www.agsnet.com

Cover Design
Sarah Bennett

Photo and Illustration Credits
Page 6, © Mug Shots/CORBIS; p. 11, Judy King Rieniets; p. 18, © David Young-Wolff/PhotoEdit; p. 41, © David Young-Wolff/PhotoEdit; p.46, Judy King Rieniets; p. 60, © Jon Riley/Getty Images; p. 75, © Philip Wallick/CORBIS; p. 78, © Brown Brothers Photographs; p. 79, © CORBIS; pp. 83–85, Patricia Isaacs/Parrot Graphics; p. 87, © The Granger Collection, New York; p. 92, © Jack Esten/Getty Images; p. 95, Patricia Isaacs/Parrot Graphics; p. 101, Joel Snyder/Portfolio Solutions; p. 105, © Joseph Sohm/ChromoSohm, Inc./CORBIS; pp. 109, 113, Judy King Rieniets; p. 115 (both), *History of Space Exploration,* © Dover Publications; pp. 124–125, Judy King Rieniets; p. 129, © David Young-Wolff/PhotoEdit; p. 133, © CORBIS

Publisher's Project Staff
Associate Director, Product Development: Teri Mathews; Senior Editor: Julie Maas; Editor: Susie Keithahn; Assistant Editor: Jan Jessup; Development Assistant: Bev Johnson; Design Manager: Nancy Condon; Senior Designer: Daren Hastings; Technical Specialist: Laura Henrichsen; Desktop Production Artist: Peggy Vlahos; Purchasing Agent: Mary Kaye Kuzma; Senior Marketing Manager/Curriculum: Brian Holl

Development and editorial services by Straight Line Editorial Development, Inc.
Art direction by Sally Brewer Lawrence

© 2003 AGS Publishing
4201 Woodland Road, Circle Pines, MN 55014-1796
800-328-2560
www.agsnet.com

AGS Publishing is a trademark of American Guidance Service, Inc.

Printed in the United States of America

Product Number 93734
ISBN 0-7854-3377-5

A 0 9 8 7 6 5 4 3

CONTENTS

CONTENTS

INTRODUCTION

Welcome!

Finding one piece of information in a world full of millions of facts can be hard! This book will show you how to use different sources of information to find the facts you need.

Here are some of the things you'll learn how to do:

- **Find facts in reference books.** An encyclopedia, a dictionary, an almanac, and an atlas all contain important information. This book will show you how to use these and other references.

- **Use the library.** The library is a valuable tool! In this book you'll learn how to use it.

- **Use print from real life.** Daily life is full of print, from magazines to newspapers to bus schedules to directions. You will learn how each kind of information is organized and how to find what you need.

- **Use the Internet wisely and safely.** This book gives important tips for finding information you need on the Internet and staying safe while doing it.

- **Think critically about what you read.** Can you trust what ads tell you? What can you learn from product labels? Is the newspaper always right? In this book you'll find out why it's important to be a critical reader and consumer.

- **Interpret information given visually.** A lot of information is given in visual ways, through pictures, maps, time lines, and diagrams. This book will show you how to interpret visual information.

With practice and a little help from this book, you'll be a master fact-finder before you know it!

TIPS FOR FINDING FACTS

■ **Choose the right source.** Think about the information source that is likely to have the information you need.

■ **Think about organization.** Before looking at the information, remember how the source you chose is organized. Should you look in the index? Should you look up a key word alphabetically? Should you look for a certain section, such as the classified ads in a newspaper?

■ **Skim and scan.** You don't have to read every word when you look for a fact. You can skim by running your eyes over the words very quickly, looking for a key fact. You can scan by reading the title and headings until you find the section you want.

■ **Don't give up.** If one source or key word doesn't get you the information you need, try another source or key word. This is especially important when using the Internet.

TIPS FOR ORGANIZING INFORMATION

Once you find the information you are looking for, how can you keep track of it? How can you avoid having to start over the next time you need to find the same kind of information?

Here are some tips for organizing information:

- **Use electronic bookmarks.** When you find a useful Web site on the Internet, use the bookmark feature to add it to your computer's memory. This will save you from having to do a key word search or having to type the address of the Web site all over again.

- **Mark important passages.** Use self-stick notes to mark pages, passages, or visuals that are important. That way you can easily find them if you need to get more information.

- **Note the source.** If you photocopy something from a book, write the title and author's name on the photocopy. That way you can give the book the right credit if you end up using those facts. Plus, if you need to find the book again, you'll know what to look for.

- **Categorize.** Sort through the information you collect and group it by type. If you are finding facts for two different papers, make two folders and label them.

- **Keep your desktop clean.** If you keep information on a computer, try to keep the files on your desktop neat. Name your folders so you know what's inside them. If you're working with paper and pen, take time to organize your books and papers every so often. It's no fun searching for lost pages!

LESSON 1   Book Parts

KEY WORD

Title page
the first page of a book

Would you buy a car without looking it over? No way! You would take a good look before saying yes.

People do the same thing with books. They look them over before they read them. Why? Simple. They don't want to read books that don't have the information they need. This lesson shows you how to look over a book.

Judging a Book by Its Cover

You may know the saying "Don't judge a book by its cover." But a cover can tell you a lot about a book.

Put a check mark next to what you might find on a book's cover:

___ title   ___ why people liked the book

___ author's name   ___ what the book is about

___ other books by the same author   ___ information about the author

If you checked everything, you're right! Covers can have all that information.

Title Page

The first page of a book is called the **title page**. It often shows these things:

- the title of the book
- the author's name
- the illustrator's name (The illustrator draws the pictures.)
- the publisher (The publisher is the company that made the book.)

Use a word in the box to name each thing on the title page below.

publisher	illustrator	title	author

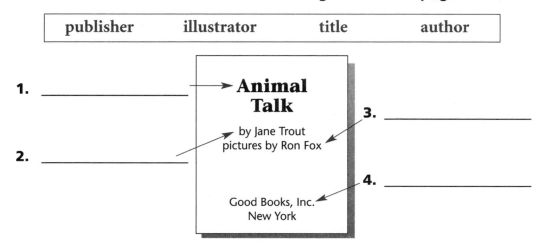

1. _____ → **Animal Talk**

        by Jane Trout
        pictures by Ron Fox

3. _____

2. _____

        Good Books, Inc.
        New York

4. _____

Copyright Page

On the back of the title page is the **copyright page**. The copyright page has

- the year the book was printed
- who owns the rights to the book
- the number of times the book has been printed

Read this copyright page. Then answer the questions.

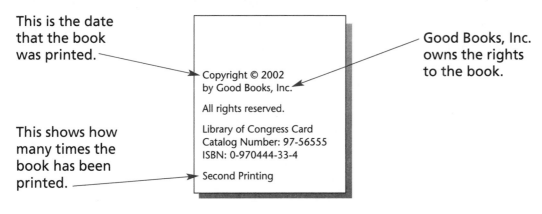
5. In what year was the book published? _____

6. How many times has the book been printed? _____

Table of Contents

Imagine you want to know about how whales talk to each other. You find a book called *Animal Talk*. Do you read the whole book and hope to find something about whales? No! You take a quick look at the **table of contents**.

- The table of contents lists all of the chapters in a book.
- The table of contents gives the page number each chapter starts on.

Read this table of contents. Then answer the questions.

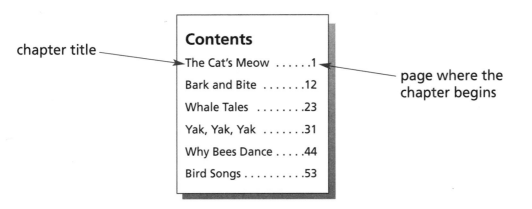

chapter title

Contents

The Cat's Meow 1
Bark and Bite 12
Whale Tales 23
Yak, Yak, Yak 31
Why Bees Dance 44
Bird Songs 53

page where the chapter begins

7. You can read about whale talk on what page? _____

8. How many chapters are in this book? _____

KEY WORDS

Copyright page
a page that lists the year a book was printed, who owns the rights to the book, and the number of times the book has been printed

Table of contents
a list of all the chapters in a book and the page number each chapter starts on

THINK ABOUT IT

The table of contents can show you how the book is organized. What do all these chapters have in common?

Index
a list of topics in a book
and the page numbers
where you can read
about the topics

Index

You looked at the cover of the book. You looked at the table of contents. Are you done looking over the book? Not yet. Don't forget the end of the book. The end of a book that contains mostly facts often has an **index**.

- An index shows topics that you can read about in a book.
- An index lists topics in alphabetical order.

Imagine you are writing a report about whale talk. What word do you look up in the index? How about the word **whales**? If you look up **whales** in the index of *Animal Talk*, you might see this:

Index

wolf, **17**

whales, **23–30**
   blue whale, **28**
   communication, **29**
   females, **25**
   humpback whale, **24**
   males, **26**

yak, **31–43**

Look at the index above. Then answer the questions.

9. Which page would you turn to in order to find out about **blue whales**?

_____

10. On which page could you find information about **male whales**?

_____

11. On which page would you probably find information about **whale talk**?

_____

LESSON 2   Using a Glossary and an Index

Using a Glossary

You will find a **glossary** at the end of many books. You may also find a glossary at the beginning or end of a chapter in a textbook. Here are some things to remember about a glossary:

- A glossary explains important words used in a chapter or book.
- Words in a glossary often relate to one big topic.
- Words in a glossary are in alphabetical order.

Here is a glossary page from *Animal Talk*.

entry word

definition

a picture to help explain the word

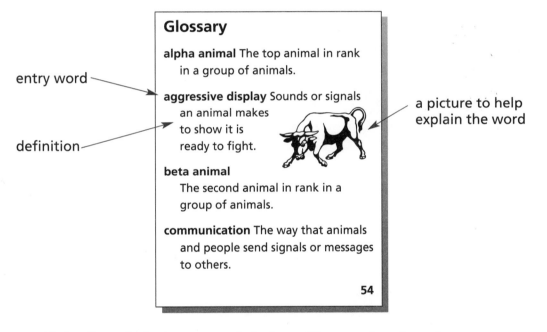

Glossary

alpha animal The top animal in rank in a group of animals.

aggressive display Sounds or signals an animal makes to show it is ready to fight.

beta animal The second animal in rank in a group of animals.

communication The way that animals and people send signals or messages to others.

54

Read the list of glossary words below. Then write them in alphabetical order on the lines.

gray squirrel   1. _____

flea   2. _____

deer   3. _____

fish   4. _____

goat   5. _____

Read this glossary page. Then answer the questions.

Glossary

data Records or notes that people collect to study something.

field study A study that people do in an animal's natural living place.

flock A group of the same kind of animal that gathers together.

habitat The place where animals and plants naturally live.

56

6. Write the meaning for the word **data** here:

_____

7. The writer wants to add the word **fox** to the glossary. Where should she put it? Fill in the correct circle.

Ⓐ between **field study** and **flock**

Ⓑ between **flock** and **habitat**

Ⓒ after **habitat**

Ⓓ before **data**

Using an Index

In Lesson 1, you learned that an index can help you find information fast. Most nonfiction books have an index. The index is at the end of a book.

- An index lists the topics in a book in alphabetical order.
- It lists the pages where you can find information about each topic.

Choosing a Topic

READING TIP

If you are looking up **George Washington,** don't look under **G**! People in an index are always listed by last name.

Imagine you want to find information on George Washington, our first president, in a book about U.S. presidents. What topic would you look up? **Washington,** right?

Topics are not always easy to figure out. Look at this example.

You have a book called *How to Understand Your Cat.* You want to know about the sounds cats make to show others they are angry. What topic should you look up in the index? Here are some choices:

Topic Search Word	Good Topic?
cats	No. It's too general. The whole book is on cats. Pick a smaller topic.
hiss	No. It's too specific. You probably won't find one particular sound that a cat makes.
sounds	Yes. This word may help you find something on sounds cats make.

Now you try. You want to look up how birds build their nests in a book about birds. Read this list of possible topics. Then write each word where you think it belongs.

robins	birds	nests

Too General	**Good Topic**	**Too Specific**
8. _____	9. _____	10. _____

Looking at Subtopics

A **subtopic** is a smaller, more specific topic within a bigger topic. For example, **howling** is a subtopic within the bigger topic **sounds**. **Howling** is a kind of sound.

11. Read each pair of words. One word in each pair is the topic. The other is a subtopic. Circle the subtopic.

sounds   barking

dogs   sheepdog

fleas   pests

KEY WORD

Subtopic
a smaller, more specific topic

STUDY TIP

Topics and subtopics can help you find information fast. Looking for topics and subtopics when you read or study can also help you organize ideas and remember key points.

Look at this index. Then answer the questions.

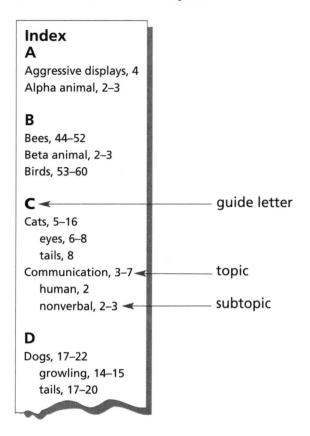

Index

A
Aggressive displays, 4
Alpha animal, 2–3

B
Bees, 44–52
Beta animal, 2–3
Birds, 53–60

C ← guide letter
Cats, 5–16
    eyes, 6–8
    tails, 8
Communication, 3–7 ← topic
    human, 2
    nonverbal, 2–3 ← subtopic

D
Dogs, 17–22
    growling, 14–15
    tails, 17–20

12. On which pages can you find information about **bees**? _____

13. How many subtopics are listed under the topic **cats**?_____

If at First You Don't Succeed

…try, try again! You may not find the information you need under the first word you look up in an index. So try another word or words.

14. Imagine you want to know what different animals show when they move their tails. You try to look up **tail** in the index, but you don't find it. Don't give up! Think of some animals that have tails. Look in the index above to find two animals that have tails. Write those two topics and page numbers here.

Topic: _____ Pages about tails: _____

Topic: _____ Pages about tails: _____

LESSON 3   Using a Dictionary, Part 1

A **dictionary** gives information about thousands of words. The words are listed in alphabetical order. A dictionary entry for a word usually includes the following:

- the **pronunciation** of the word (how to say it)
- the part of speech (noun, verb, or other)
- other forms of the word
- meanings of the word
- sample sentences
- the history of the word

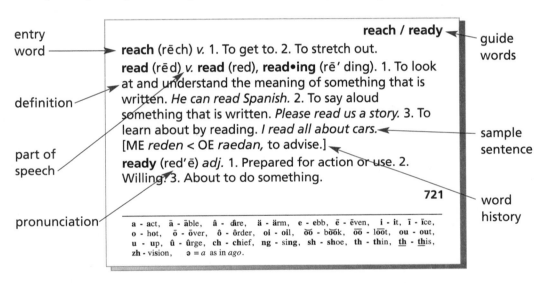

entry word
definition
part of speech
pronunciation

reach / ready
guide words

reach (rēch) *v.* 1. To get to. 2. To stretch out.
read (rēd) *v.* **read** (red), **read•ing** (rē′ ding). 1. To look at and understand the meaning of something that is written. *He can read Spanish.* 2. To say aloud something that is written. *Please read us a story.* 3. To learn about by reading. *I read all about cars.* [ME *reden* < OE *raedan,* to advise.]
ready (red′ē) *adj.* 1. Prepared for action or use. 2. Willing. 3. About to do something.

721

sample sentence
word history

a - act, ā - āble, â - dâre, ä - ärm, e - ebb, ē - ēven, i - it, ī - īce,
o - hot, ō - ōver, ô - ôrder, oi - oil, ŏŏ - bŏŏk, ōō - lōōt, ou - out,
u - up, û - ûrge, ch - chief, ng - sing, sh - shoe, th - thin, th - this,
zh - vision,   ə = *a* as in *ago.*

Guide Words

Guide words appear at the top of a dictionary page. They help you find a word fast. The first guide word is the first word on the page. The second guide word is the last word on the page.

1. Look at the guide words on the dictionary page above. Which is the last entry word on the dictionary page? ____ reach ____ ready

Write these words in alphabetical order under the correct guide words.

brace	be	box	bay

bath / beach   bowl / brag

2. _____   **4.** _____

3. _____   **5.** _____

KEY WORDS

Noun
a word that names a person, place, or thing

Abbreviation
a short form of a word

Adjective
a word that describes a person, place, or thing

Adverb
a word that describes an action

Verb
a word that names an action

WRITING TIP

Do you see the plural spelling of **fez**? (It's after the abbreviation **pl.**) The dictionary can show you how to form irregular plurals, such as **fezzes**.

Word Spy

Imagine you are a new spy. You are working on your first top secret job. Your boss hands you these instructions.

> **Top Secret**
> - Go to the park. Look for the man in the red fez.
> - Stroll up to the man.
> - Tell him, "That's a nice chapeau."
> - He will give you a missive. Take the missive back to your boss.

You want to do a good job, but there is a problem. You do not know the meanings of the words **fez, stroll, chapeau,** and **missive**. You begin to worry. Then you have an idea. Use a dictionary! You run home and pull the dictionary from its shelf.

Not-So-Secret Meanings

You look up the word **fez**. This is what you see.

> **fez** (fez) *n., pl.* **fez•zes**. A man's felt cap. It is in the shape of a flat cone. It is usually red.

Read the definition above. Fill in the circle next to the correct answer.

6. A fez is a kind of _____.

Ⓐ hat   Ⓒ shoe

Ⓑ vest   Ⓓ belt

Do you see the letter **n** before the definition? Circle the letter **n**. The letter **n** tells you the word **fez** is a noun. The **n** is an abbreviation for **noun**. An **abbreviation** is a short form of a word.

7. Match each abbreviation with the word it stands for:

n.   **adjective** (a word that describes a person, place, or thing)

v.   **noun** (a person, place, or thing)

adj.   **adverb** (a word that describes an action)

adv.   **verb** (a word that names an action)

How to Say It

The note tells you to say, "That's a nice chapeau" to the other spy. How do you find out how to say "chapeau"? You look up **chapeau** in the dictionary. This is what you see:

> **cha•peau** (sha-pō′) *n., pl.* **-peaus** (-pōz′) A hat. [*Fr. chapel* < *Lat. cappa.*]

Circle the pronunciation of *chapeau*. Say it aloud.

8. The vowel sound in **sha** sounds like the vowel sound in the word _____.

Ⓐ shack

Ⓑ ship

Ⓒ shape

Ⓓ shut

9. The vowel sound in **pō** sounds like the vowel sound in the word _____.

Ⓐ pea

Ⓑ note

Ⓒ bus

Ⓓ cow

READING TIP

Here are some tips to help you read word histories in dictionary entries:

< = comes from

Fr. = French

Lat. = Latin

How to Use It

When you look up the word **stroll,** you see something odd. **Stroll** can be a noun or a verb. Look at the sample sentences. They show how to use the word as a verb or a noun.

> **stroll** (strōl) *v.* **strolled, stroll•ing, strolls**. To go for a slow walk. *I strolled through the park.* —*n.* A slow walk. *Let's take a long stroll.*

10. Write the sample sentence for the noun form of **stroll**:

_____

11. The dictionary lists words by their simplest form. Which of the following would you look up to find the meaning of the word **spies**?

Ⓐ spying

Ⓑ spied

Ⓒ spy

Ⓓ spies

On Your Own

12. Look up the word **missive**. What is the spy going to bring back to his boss?

Ⓐ a bomb

Ⓑ a bag of money

Ⓒ a note

Ⓓ a map

LESSON 4   Using a Dictionary, Part 2

KEY WORDS

Context clue
nearby words that help
you figure out a word's
meaning in a sentence

Definition
the meaning of a word

Dictionaries often list more than one meaning for a word. When you look up a new word, how do you find the meaning you need?

Step 1: Look at how the word is used in your sentence.
Step 2: Look for **context clues**. These are nearby words that help you figure out the word's meaning in the sentence.
Step 3: Look for clues in the dictionary **definitions**.
Step 4: Choose a definition and test it.

Choosing the Right Meaning

Let's try these steps out on a word you know. Imagine you read these sentences in a story:

I took out my new cell phone to call a cab. New cell phones usually **work**. Mine did not. I looked for a pay phone.

Imagine you aren't sure what **work** means here. You look up the word in the dictionary. This is what you see:

> **work** (wûrk) *n.* 1. An effort made to do or get something. 2. Something that is done or has to be done. 3. The place where one does one's job. —*v.* 4. To do something to make money. 5. To put forth effort to do or get something. 6. To function properly.

Wow! There are a lot of definitions. Should you give up? No! Use the four steps:

Step 1: Look at how the word is used.

Read this sentence:

New cell phones usually work.

1. In this sentence, **work** is _____. Check one.

____ a thing   ____ an action

Did you choose action? You're right! **Work** is a verb in the sentence. So look for the **v** in the dictionary entry for **work**. See it? Circle the letter **v**.

Now you can ignore definitions 1, 2, and 3. Those definitions are for nouns. You only have three definitions to choose from.

Step 2: Look for context clues around the word.

Read the sentences again:

I took out my new cell phone to call a cab. Most new cell phones work. Mine did not. I looked for a pay phone.

2–3. Here are some context clues that help you understand how **work** is used in this sentence. Read the context clues. Match each clue with what it tells you. One is done for you.

Context Clue	What It Tells You
phone to call a cab	**Work** is the verb in this sentence. It is the only word that names an action.
New cell phones usually work.	The cell phone did not function.
Mine did not.	Someone needed to use a phone.

Step 3: Look for clues in the dictionary definitions.

Read this sentence again:

Most new cell phones work.

4. Which definition below seems to be the best definition of **work** in the sentence? Check one.

_____ to do something to make money

_____ to put forth effort to do or get something

_____ to function properly

Step 4: Choose a definition and test it out.

By now you have an idea that definition 6 is the one you need. Let's test it out.

5. Complete this sentence with some words from definition 6 on page 18.
New cell phones usually _____.

Does that make sense? Congratulations! You have picked the best definition for **work** in the original sentence.

On Your Own

Read this sentence:

The test day loomed before me.

The word **loomed** tells something about a test day, so you decide it is important. You look it up. Here is what you see:

> **loom** (lo͞om) *n.* A machine used to weave thread into cloth. —*v.* **loomed, loom•ing** 1. To appear as large and dangerous. *A large shape loomed in the fog.* 2. To be about to happen. *The beginning of the school year loomed ahead.*

6. Read the sentence that **loomed** is in. What job is **loomed** doing in the sentence? Fill in the correct circle.

   Ⓐ It names a thing. It is a noun.

   Ⓑ It tells about an action. It is a verb.

   Ⓒ It describes a thing. It is an adjective.

   Ⓓ It describes an action. It is an adverb.

7. Which definition of **loom** makes the most sense in context? Fill in the correct circle.

   Ⓐ a machine used to weave thread into cloth

   Ⓑ to appear as large and dangerous

   Ⓒ to be about to happen

   Ⓓ none of the above

LESSON 5   Using a Thesaurus

Do you ever repeat the same word over and over when you write? Do you wish you had another word to use? A **thesaurus** can help you add life to your writing. It can help you find just the right word.

- A **thesaurus** shows synonyms for words. It sometimes has antonyms too.
- A **synonym** is a word that has almost the same meaning as another word.
- An **antonym** is a word that means the opposite of another word.

KEY WORDS

Thesaurus
a book that lists synonyms and antonyms of words

Synonym
a word that has almost the same meaning as another word

Antonym
a word that means the opposite of another word

Read a Sample Thesaurus Entry

Here is what you might see in a thesaurus under the word **big**:

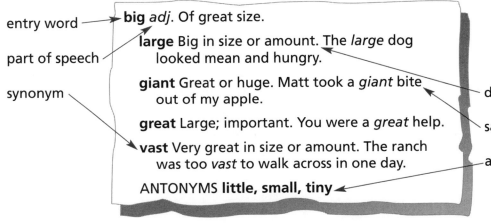

entry word → **big** *adj.* Of great size.
part of speech
large Big in size or amount. The *large* dog looked mean and hungry. ← definition
giant Great or huge. Matt took a *giant* bite out of my apple.
synonym
great Large; important. You were a *great* help. ← sample sentence
vast Very great in size or amount. The ranch was too *vast* to walk across in one day. ← antonyms
ANTONYMS **little, small, tiny**

1. Which synonym for **big** also means important? Fill in the correct circle.

   Ⓐ large   Ⓒ great

   Ⓑ giant   Ⓓ vast

2. Read this sentence:

   It took us all day to cross the vast desert.

   Is **vast** a good word choice in this sentence?

   ____ yes, good choice   ____ no, bad choice

Add Color to Your Writing

Imagine you are writing a fiction story. You have used the word **say** too many times. So you look up **say** in the thesaurus. Here's what you see:

> **Say**
>
> **chant** Say as a group.
>
> **exclaim** Say with strong emotion.
>
> **mutter** Say in a low, unclear way.
>
> **speak** Talk in an ordinary way.
>
> **state** Tell or explain in words.

3. Fill in the circle next to the best word. The coach _____ each rule clearly.

Ⓐ muttered   Ⓒ stated

Ⓑ exclaimed   Ⓓ chanted

4. Fill in the circle next to the best word. "That isn't fair," Tom _____ softly. He was unhappy, but he didn't want the coach to hear him.

Ⓐ muttered   Ⓒ chanted

Ⓑ talked   Ⓓ exclaimed

Two Kinds of Thesauruses

A thesaurus may look like a dictionary, or it may have two parts:

- an index that lists words in alphabetical order and gives their subject numbers
- a section that groups word entries by subject and subject number

If you look up the word **wave** in the index, you may see this:

> **wave**
>
> greet, 410.11
>
> sea, 571.1

5. Which word would you look up in the subject section to find other words that mean "a wave on the ocean"? Check one.

____ greet   ____ sea

LESSON 6   Electronic Dictionaries and Books

For many years people used computers mostly to type letters and store information. Today, people use computers in many different ways. This lesson will show you some ways to use your computer to find useful information.

Electronic Dictionaries

There are two kinds of dictionaries you can use on a computer.

- **CD-ROM dictionaries** are located on computer hard drives or on CD-ROMs. A CD-ROM looks like a music CD.
- **Online dictionaries** are ones you can use over the Internet.

Each electronic dictionary is a little different from others. But most share some things in common.

KEY WORDS

CD-ROM dictionary
a dictionary located on a compact disc and accessed through a computer

Online dictionary
a dictionary located on the Internet and accessed through a Web browser on a computer

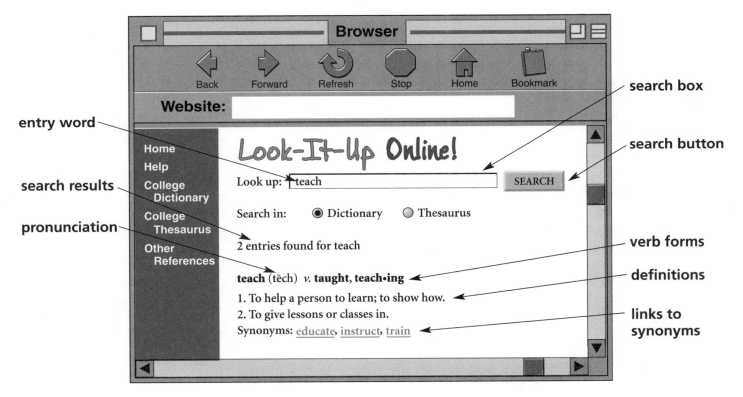

Look at the computer screen on page 23 to answer these questions.

1. How many entries were found for the word **teach**? _____

2. Write two other forms of the verb **teach**:

_____

3. How many links are there to synonyms for **teach**? _____

Looking Up Words

Electronic dictionaries are very helpful if you aren't sure how to spell a word. They also help you find other forms of a word.

For example, let's say you aren't sure how to spell **ability**—is it spelled **ability** or **abilaty**? Type the first part of the word plus * in the search box. The dictionary will find all the words that start with the letters you typed.

Step 1: You type in **abil***.

Step 2: You see the search results.

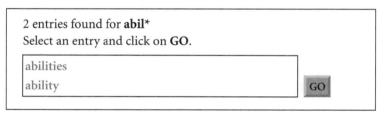

4. How many words beginning with **abil** did the dictionary find?

_____

5. Circle the correct spelling of the word: ability   abilaty

Online Books

Did you know that you can find books online? Here is what a search box for an online book may look like.

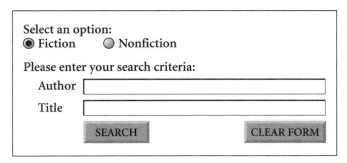

6. You want to find *The Red Pony* by John Steinbeck. How can you find it?

Ⓐ Type **The Red Pony** in the author box.

Ⓑ Type **The Red Pony** in the title box.

Ⓒ Type **John Steinbeck** in the title box.

Ⓓ Type **Pony** in the author box and **Steinbeck** in the title box.

Some Internet sites charge you money to read their books. But there are many books you can read for free. If you decide to read a book online, here are some things to remember:

• Use the mouse and the scroll bar to see more text as you read.
• Stop now and then to check that you understand what you are reading.
• If you are confused about something, reread or read ahead. Look for information that will clear up your confusion.
• Take breaks to rest your eyes and stretch your body.

Try It Out

Now you are ready to try out some computer searches on your own. You may have a computer at home. If you don't, go to a computer lab at your school or local library.

• Find an electronic computer dictionary. Look up the word **altruism**. Write down the definitions you find.
• Look up **Aesop's fables** online. Read one fable online. Be prepared to share the message of the fable with the class.

Part A   Book Parts

Read this title page. Then write words from the box on the lines to identify the parts of the title page.

publisher	city where published	title	author

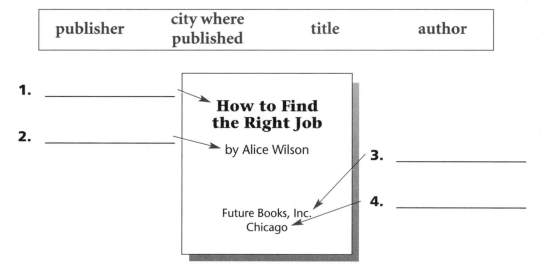

1. _____

2. _____

3. _____

4. _____

How to Find the Right Job

by Alice Wilson

Future Books, Inc.
Chicago

Read this copyright page and table of contents. Then answer the questions below.

Copyright © 2002
by Future Books, Inc.

All rights reserved.

Library of Congress Card Catalog
Number: 97-53525
ISBN: 0-970334-22-1

Third Printing

Contents

Resumes 1

Want Ads 22

Job Applications 41

Interviews 63

5. What year was the book published? _____

6. What page should you turn to for facts about want ads? _____

7. How many chapters are in this book? _____

Searching for Words and Topics

Part B

Read these dictionary entry words. Then put them in alphabetical order under the correct guide words.

brace	batter	be	box	bracket	bay

bath / beach   **bowl / brag**

1. _____   **4.** _____

2. _____   **5.** _____

3. _____   **6.** _____

Imagine that this is part of an index page from a book on wild animals in national parks. Write each word listed in the box below where it belongs in the index.

grizzly	bison	badgers	Kodiak

alligators

7. _____

bears

    black

8. _____

9. _____

beavers

10. _____

Part C   Where to Find Word Meanings

Read these sentences. Choose the information that best completes each sentence. Fill in the circle.

1. You want to know the meaning of a word in a science book. You should turn to the _____ at the back of the book.

   Ⓐ thesaurus   Ⓒ dictionary

   Ⓑ title page   Ⓓ glossary

2. The purpose of a thesaurus is to help you _____.

   Ⓐ look up a key word in a history book

   Ⓑ find other choices for a word

   Ⓒ see how to pronounce a word

   Ⓓ look up a word's history

Read this sentence. Then answer the questions.

The lake was fed by several springs.

3. In the sentence above, **springs** probably means _____.

   Ⓐ a season of the year   Ⓒ water coming up from the ground

   Ⓑ coils made of wire   Ⓓ jumps

4. Look up **spring** in a dictionary. What guide words do you see at the top of the page?

   _____ and _____

5. How many entries are given for **spring**? _____

6. Which meaning is being used in the sentence above? Write it here.

   _____

   _____

Look It Up

Find a book you are reading for school, such as a science or social studies textbook. (Or use this study skills book.) Write down the following information for the book.

1. Title: _____

2. Author: _____

3. Copyright date: _____

4. Name of publisher: _____

5. How many chapters does it have? _____

6. Does it have a glossary? ____ yes ____ no

7. Does it have an index? ____ yes ____ no

8. Write one topic you can find in the index: _____

9. Find a topic that has a subtopic listed under it. Write the topic and subtopic here:
   Topic: _____

   Subtopic: _____

STUDY TIP

You can use key term lists or glossaries in textbooks to help you study for tests. First, cover the definitions and review the terms to see which ones you know. Then, study the ones you don't know!

Fill in the circle next to the best answer for each question.

10. What do you need to know about a book to look it up online?

    Ⓐ the copyright date

    Ⓒ the author's middle name

    Ⓑ the publisher

    Ⓓ the title

11. You want to look up a book by a poet you like. You know her first name is Maya. You aren't sure if she spells her last name Angeloo or Angelou. What can you type in the author search box to see a list of authors whose last names start with Angel?

    Ⓐ Maya

    Ⓒ Angel-something

    Ⓑ Angel, M Somebody

    Ⓓ Angel*

TECH TIP

You can search for an electronic book by author, title, or subject. If you don't know all of a title or author's name, just type the part that you know into the search box.

LESSON 7

Test-Taking Strategies

Tests check what you know. You may take a test at school or at work. In this lesson, you will learn some tricks to help you do better on tests.

Getting Ready

These tips tell you how to get ready for a test.

Several Days Before the Test	The Night Before the Test	The Day of the Test
• Reread parts of the book. • Take notes on key facts. • Make note cards for important ideas. • Study with a friend. • Do not wait until the last minute to study!	• Look over the headings in the book. Tell yourself what each section talks about. • Read over your notes and note cards. • Try not to worry. You'll do well if you have studied. • Get a good night's sleep.	• Eat a good breakfast. • Make sure you have what you need for the test (pencils, scrap paper). • If you have any questions, ask them before the test begins. • Try to relax.

STUDY TIP

As you study in the days and nights before a test, keep asking yourself questions about the topic. For example, if you're studying for a test about killer whales, ask yourself: How big are they? How do they get their food? Where do they live? Are they dangerous to humans?

Test Prep Pop Quiz

Read the sentences below. Write Yes next to the sentences that tell what you should do to get ready for a test. Write No next to the sentences that tell what you shouldn't do.

1. _____ It is best to wait until the last minute to study for a test.

2. _____ Use notes and note cards to help you remember facts.

3. _____ Try studying with a friend.

4. _____ Stay up as late as you can the night before the test.

5. _____ Read over your notes and note cards a day before the test.

6. _____ Skip breakfast on the day of the test—it will only make you sleepy.

7. _____ Ask questions before the test begins.

8. _____ Whatever you do, don't relax. Being nervous will help you.

Budgeting Time

Many tests are timed. This means that you must finish in a set amount of time. For timed tests, make a time plan before you start. Do not worry if other students finish before you do.

Use what you know about timed tests to answer these questions.

9. You start a test at 1:00. You must finish by 2:00. At about what time should you be halfway done? _____

10. You have 20 minutes to finish a 10-question test. About how much time should you spend on each question? _____ minutes

I have 30 minutes to finish this test. It has 20 questions. I will try to finish half of the questions in 15 minutes. That means I need to finish the first 10 questions by 10:20. I'll check the clock as I work.

Reading Directions

Most tests have directions that tell you what to do. Be sure to read the directions slowly and carefully before you begin. Every word counts! There are key words in each set of directions that tell you exactly what to do. Some key words are **read, write, answer, draw, circle, underline,** and **fill in**. In the example directions below, the key words have been circled for you.

Example

Read the following paragraph. Then circle each misspelled word and write it correctly in the margin.

Find and circle the key words in the directions below.

11–12. Underline the verbs in these sentences. Then write those words in the blanks.

Now carefully read and follow the directions below.

Read each question. Write your answer on the line next to the question. Skip the first question.

13. What is the largest city in America? _____

14. Which sport do you like best? _____

15. What is your favorite sports team? _____

LESSON 8 — Multiple-Choice Questions

KEY WORD

Multiple-choice question
a question that gives a set of answer choices

Many tests give you a set of answer choices for each question. These questions are called **multiple-choice questions**. They can be tricky.

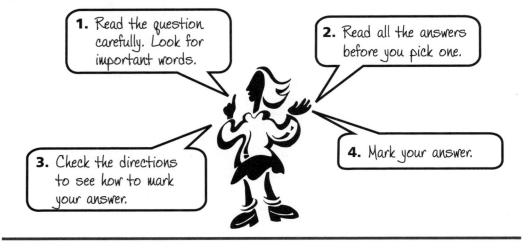

1. Read the question carefully. Look for important words.

2. Read all the answers before you pick one.

3. Check the directions to see how to mark your answer.

4. Mark your answer.

Look for Direction Words

Read the directions and circle the words that tell you how to mark your answer. Then answer the questions.

Fill in the circle next to the best answer.

1. What is a jet?
   Ⓐ a cactus
   Ⓑ a bird
   Ⓒ a plane
   Ⓓ a robot

2. Who grows crops?
   Ⓐ a camper
   Ⓑ a cobbler
   Ⓒ a runner
   Ⓓ a farmer

Choose the word that has almost the same meaning as the underlined word. Circle the letter next to the correct answer.

3. gaze
   Ⓐ look
   Ⓑ slump
   Ⓒ change
   Ⓓ work

4. speak
   Ⓐ leap
   Ⓑ compile
   Ⓒ talk
   Ⓓ think

Eliminate Wrong Answers

What if you aren't sure about an answer? Here's how to make a good choice. Read over the answer choices again. You will see some that you know are wrong. Get rid of those choices. You will then have a better chance of choosing the correct answer. This is called **educated guessing**.

For the multiple-choice questions below, draw a line through the answers you know are wrong. The first one has been done for you.

Where would you go to see wild animals?

- Ⓐ ~~airport~~
- Ⓑ ~~subway~~
- Ⓒ ~~garage~~
- Ⓓ zoo

5. Which animal eats other animals?

- Ⓐ cow
- Ⓑ lion
- Ⓒ pig
- Ⓓ horse

6. Which animal lives in the ocean?

- Ⓐ bear
- Ⓑ tuna
- Ⓒ mink
- Ⓓ frog

7. Which animal has fur?

- Ⓐ bird
- Ⓑ fish
- Ⓒ turtle
- Ⓓ tiger

KEY WORD

Educated guessing
eliminating answer choices that are clearly wrong and making the best choice from the remaining answer choices

Try It Out

Answer these test questions. Remember to look for directions that tell you how to mark your answers. Remember to eliminate the wrong answers first. Circle the letter next to the correct answer.

8. What is batter used for?

- Ⓐ test
- Ⓑ writing
- Ⓒ maps
- Ⓓ cake

9. Which one can't fly?

- Ⓐ a bat
- Ⓑ a slug
- Ⓒ a bird
- Ⓓ a bee

Choose the word that has almost the same meaning as the underlined word. Fill in the circle next to the correct answer.

10. nap

- Ⓐ nip
- Ⓑ sleep
- Ⓒ tap
- Ⓓ make

11. divide

- Ⓐ take
- Ⓑ dive
- Ⓒ give
- Ⓓ split

LESSON 9   Fill In the Blank

Some multiple-choice tests ask you to fill in a blank with one of the answer choices. How do you choose the best answer? First, try to complete the sentence without looking at the answer choices. Then read the sentence, using each answer choice to fill in the blank. Choose the answer that works best. Look at the sentence below.

Dan listens to his favorite _____ on CD.

    food   color

    tunes   car

> I think the answer is **music**. I'll read the sentence using each answer just to make sure. **Food** and **color** don't work because you can't listen to **food** or **color**. **Car** is wrong because you can't put a **car** on CD! **Tunes** makes sense. **Tunes** is another word for **music**. I thought so!

Practice Filling In the Blanks

Now fill in the blank to complete each sentence.

1. The _____ was elected to lead the city.

    mayor   country

    school   infant

2. Sam's 40¢ is made up of three dimes and _____ nickels.

    one   two

    three   eight

Read the passage. Then complete each sentence by filling in the blank.

There are about 360 different kinds of sharks. Only about 50 of these are dangerous to people. Sharks live in oceans and eat meat, and their most common enemy is larger sharks. The world's largest shark is the whale shark—it can grow to be 40 feet long. The smallest sharks may be only 6 inches long!

3. This passage tells about _____.

sharks   whales

dangers   meat

4. About _____ kinds of sharks are dangerous to people.

50   40

360   6

Do Easy Questions First

Most tests have questions that are hard for even the best students. But test questions do not always get harder as you go along. Easy questions are usually spread throughout the test.

Answer these questions. Skip the hard ones and answer the easy ones. Then go back and finish the questions you skipped.

Fill in the circle next to the best answer.

> I will skip the questions I am unsure of. I will answer the questions I know the answers to. After that, I will go back and answer the questions I skipped. If I hit a few hard questions in a row, I will **not** stop working. There will be easier ones ahead.

5. A shirt is on sale for 25% off the marked price. The marked price is $52.40. What is the sale price?

Ⓐ $45.35

Ⓑ $20.50

Ⓒ $39.30

Ⓓ $41.65

6. Which word does not mean the same as **small**?

Ⓐ tiny   Ⓒ short

Ⓑ little   Ⓓ huge

7. What is the next number: 2, 4, 6, 8, 8, 6, 4, ___?

Ⓐ 6   Ⓒ 2

Ⓑ 4   Ⓓ 8

8. _____ is a U.S. state.

Ⓐ America   Ⓒ Maine

Ⓑ India   Ⓓ Canada

LESSON 10 Responding to Writing Prompts

KEY WORDS

Writing prompt
an instruction that tells you what information to include when answering a question with a written response

Topic sentence
the opening sentence of a written response to a question

Expository writing
writing that tells about a real-life topic or explains something

Some tests have questions that you must answer by writing sentences. These questions usually give you a **writing prompt** that tells you what information you should include. These kinds of questions call for you to think carefully.

1. Look for key words in the question. Try to use these words in your answer.

2. Jot down notes and plan out your writing.

3. Always write complete sentences.

4. Budget your time so you don't run out.

5. Make sure to read over your answers and fix mistakes.

Writing Short Written Responses

A short written response is made up of a few sentences. Write as many sentences as you need to explain your answer. You might need two, three, five, or seven sentences—it doesn't matter, as long as you answer the prompt. Here is an example.

Writing Prompt: Would you like to go bungee jumping? Write a short response explaining why or why not.

Sample Answer: Yes, I would like to go bungee jumping. This sport looks scary and exciting. Also, I like trying new things.

The opening sentence is called the **topic sentence**. It sets up the rest of your answer. Try to use key words from the question in the topic sentence. The sentences after the topic sentence should give details or facts that support the topic sentence.

Expository Writing—Short Response

Expository writing tells about a real-life topic or explains something. Read the next example of expository writing.

Writing Prompt: Think about your favorite kind of music. Write a paragraph explaining why you like it. Give reasons to support your answer.

Sample Answer: My favorite kind of music is techno. I like it because it's fun to move with the music and dance. Also, DJs are always coming up with new beats. It's the coolest music around.

Now use what you know about expository writing to respond to the writing prompt.

Writing Prompt: Think about a place that you would like to visit. Write a paragraph explaining why you would like to go there. Give reasons to support your answer.

1. Your Answer: _____

_____

_____

_____

_____

_____

_____

Narrative Writing—Short Response

Narrative writing tells a story. A personal narrative is a story about yourself. Read the example of narrative writing below.

Writing Prompt: Write a short personal narrative about a trip you took to a distant place.

Sample Answer: I went to visit my relatives in Spain when I was 12 years old. The flight was very long, but at last we landed in Madrid. Then we took a train to my aunt's house in a small town near the coast. The little white houses with tile roofs were very pretty. We visited street fairs and took a trip to a nice beach. I played soccer with my cousins. I didn't want to leave Spain. I hope to go back someday soon.

Now use what you know about narrative writing to respond to the writing prompt on the next page.

KEY WORD

Narrative writing
writing that tells a story

Opening paragraph
a first paragraph that tells what you are writing about

Body
one or more paragraphs in a written response giving details that explain the answer

Ending paragraph
a last paragraph that sums up what is being said in a written response

Concluding sentence
the last sentence of an ending paragraph

Outline
an organized list of main ideas and details

Writing Prompt: Write a short personal narrative about a time when you were proud to finish something.

2. Your Answer: _____

_____

_____

_____

_____

Writing Longer Written Responses

Some test questions call for you to write a longer response made up of three to five paragraphs. The key to writing longer answers is to **make a plan**.

- The **opening paragraph** tells what you are writing about. It has a topic sentence.
- The **body** of the answer has one or more paragraphs. These paragraphs give details that explain your answer.
- The **ending paragraph** sums up what you are saying. It should end with a **concluding sentence**.

Making an Outline

An **outline** is an organized list of main ideas and details. Making an outline before you write can help you organize your thoughts. Read the writing prompt below. Then read the outline to see how the author organized her thoughts.

Writing Prompt: Think about someone you admire. Write several paragraphs describing this person and why you admire him or her. Give reasons to support your answer.

Outline
I. Opening paragraph
A. Topic sentence: I admire my mother, Beth Smith
B. admire new things every day
II. Explanation
A. as a lawyer (public defender)
1. helps people
2. works hard
B. as a mom
1. helps with homework
2. gives advice
III. Ending paragraph
A. great woman
B. hope to be like her

Answer each question by filling in the circle next to the best answer.

3. Where in the outline should the writer add this detail: **"cares about people she defends"**?

Ⓐ under I. A. Ⓒ under II. B.

Ⓑ under II. A. Ⓓ under III. B.

4. Where in the outline should she put this detail: **"is a good friend to me"**?

Ⓐ under I. A. Ⓒ under II. B.

Ⓑ under II. A. Ⓓ under III. B.

Now read the response the author wrote, based on her outline.

The person I admire most is my mother, Beth Smith. I've known her all my life, but every day I still find new things to admire about her.

My mother is a kind of lawyer known as a public defender. She helps people in need who can't afford to pay for a lawyer. Her job does not pay a lot, but she still works hard every day to defend people.

The thing I love most about my mom is that she always has time for me. No matter how busy she is, she finds time to help me with my homework. She also gives great advice and treats me like a friend.

Beth Smith is a great woman, and I admire her very much. She is a good lawyer, but an even better mother. One day I hope to be like her.

5. Now read this writing prompt. Create an outline (below and on the next page) to plan your answer. Refer to the example outline on page 38.

Writing Prompt: Think about a person you admire. Write four paragraphs explaining why you admire him or her. Include details that will help your reader understand why this person is special.

Outline

I. Opening paragraph

   A. Topic sentence: _____

    _____

   B. Details: _____

    _____

II. Explanation

   A. _____

     1. _____

     2. _____

WRITING TIP

When you reread your writing, make sure that

- Every sentence is complete.
- You have used capital letters correctly.

B. ______________________________

1. ______________________________

2. ______________________________

III. Ending paragraph

A. ______________________________

____

B. ______________________________

____

(Remember your concluding sentence!)

6. Now write your complete response below. Use the outline as a guide.

Title: ______________________________

Opening paragraph: ______________________________

____

____

____

____

Second paragraph: ______________________________

____

____

____

____

Third paragraph: ______________________________

____

____

____

____

Ending paragraph: ______________________________

____

____

____

____

LESSON 11   Real-World Test: Getting a Driver's License

Sometimes you may have to take a test outside of school. For example, you must pass both a driving test and a written test before you can drive. Every driver needs to learn the rules of the road and be tested on them. The test-taking skills you have learned so far can help you pass the test and get your driver's license.

Steps for Getting Your Driver's License

The laws for getting a driver's license are different in every state. The basic steps are the same though.

Step 1: Get a Learner's Permit
Study the rules of the road in your state. When you know these rules well enough, you can take a written test. If you pass, you get a **learner's permit** that says you are learning to drive. You can drive, as long as you are with a licensed driver who is old enough. (Check the rules in your state to find out how old the driver must be, as well as any other rules.)

Step 2: Take Driver's Ed
Once you can drive, most states call for you to take a **driver's education** training class. In this class, you practice driving with a teacher. You get a form when you finish the driver's education class. With a learner's permit and a driver's education form, you can take your driver's license test in most states.

Step 3: Practice Driving
Some states make you wait 6 to 9 months after you get your learner's permit before you can take your driver's license test. This is so you will have plenty of time to practice driving. In some states, you need to prove that you have driven for at least 30 hours before you can take the driver's license test.

Step 4: Take the Driver's License Test
Most states have special places where driver's license tests are given. You may have to take a written test, an eye test, and a driving test. You must take the driving test with a state official to show that you know how to control a car.

KEY WORDS

Learner's permit
a paper that states that you are learning to drive

Driver's education
a training class that prepares you to take a driver's license test

THINK ABOUT IT

Do you think there are too many rules for getting a driver's license? Why or why not? What do you think would happen if there were no rules for getting a driver's license?

Here's what you should bring to the driver's license test:

- your learner's permit and driver's education form
- a licensed driver (Remember—you can't drive there unless you have your license.)
- a car or truck in good shape

Step 5: Get Your License
If you pass the driver's license test, you will be given a paper license. The state will mail you your real license. If you fail your test, you need to set up another time to take the test and start practicing again.

What Have You Learned So Far?

Use what you know about getting your driver's license to finish these items.

1. Write a number from 1 to 5 in front of each step below. Show the order of the steps.

    _____ **A** Take a driving test with a state official.

    _____ **B** Get your license in the mail. Woohoo!

    _____ **C** Take a driver's ed class.

    _____ **D** Get your learner's permit.

    _____ **E** Practice driving.

2. Are the laws for getting a driver's license the same in every state?
    ___ yes   ___ no

3. What three kinds of tests may drivers-in-training have to take?

    _____

    _____

    _____

4. What do drivers-in-training need to bring to their driver's license test?

    _____

    _____

    _____

5. What two things do you need to do if you fail your driver's license test?

    _____

    _____

Learn Some Rules of the Road

Here is a sample page from a state driver's handbook. It talks about some driving rules and laws. Read it carefully.

RULES OF THE ROAD

Do not:
- Drive with your car or truck so packed that you can't see ahead or to the sides of it.
- Let a person ride in the bed of your pickup truck unless the bed has seats and seat belts.
- Tow anyone who is riding a bicycle, in a wagon, on roller skates, on a sled, or on skis.
- Sound your horn unless it is as a warning.
- Wear a headset over, or earplugs in, both your ears.

SIGNS

The shape of a sign gives you a clue about its meaning. Here are the common shapes used:

- The eight-sided, red STOP sign means that you must make a full stop. Check for people or cars. Wait until it is safe before going forward.

- The three-sided, red YIELD sign means slow down or stop to let people, cars, or bikes pass before you go ahead.

- Square, red-and-white signs tell you about rules you must follow. For example, the DO NOT ENTER sign tells you there is danger ahead because cars will be coming toward you.

- The WRONG WAY sign may be with the DO NOT ENTER sign. It tells you not to drive this way because you'll be going against the flow of traffic.

- A red circle with a red line through it always means no. The picture inside the circle shows what you cannot do. The sign may be shown with words under it.

- Diamond-shaped signs warn drivers of road problems and dangers ahead. This sign tells you there's a dangerous curve ahead.

- SPEED LIMIT signs tell you how fast you can go. No matter what the speed limit is, though, never go faster than is safe.

Take a Sample Test

Now answer these questions from a driver's license test. Use the information from the sample handbook, plus what you know about written tests. Put a check mark on the line next to the correct answer.

6. It is OK to wear headphones over both of your ears when driving.

___ true ___ false

7. It is OK to let a person ride in the bed of your pickup truck if he or she is sitting in a seat and using a seat belt.

___ true ___ false

Fill in the circle next to the best answer.

8. You should only sound your horn _____.

Ⓐ as a joke

Ⓒ at a curb

Ⓑ in a truck

Ⓓ as a warning

9. To **yield** means to _____.

Ⓐ let others go first

Ⓒ go the wrong way

Ⓑ stop at a stop sign

Ⓓ pass a driver's test

10. What does a red circle with a red line through it always mean?

Ⓐ wrong way

Ⓒ no

Ⓑ yield

Ⓓ curved road

11. What does this sign mean?

Ⓐ dangerous curve

Ⓑ stop

Ⓒ no U-turn

Ⓓ do not enter

12. A red stop sign has _____ sides.

Ⓐ 3

Ⓒ 2

Ⓑ 4

Ⓓ 8

LESSON 12   Taking an Online Test

More and more tests are being given on computers. A test taken on a computer is called an **online test**. An online test may ask the kinds of questions you have learned about in this chapter—multiple choice, fill in the blank, and questions that ask for a written response.

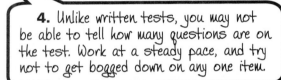

1. Get to know the computer you are using before the test starts. Get to know the keyboard and the mouse. Make sure you can read the screen.

3. Be extra careful when taking an online test. Sometimes you can't go back and check or change your answers.

2. Make sure you know how to move through the test. How do you go forward to the next question? Can you go back to change an answer? If so, how? If you are not sure, ask someone.

4. Unlike written tests, you may not be able to tell how many questions are on the test. Work at a steady pace, and try not to get bogged down on any one item.

Online Test Directions

Before you begin an online test, always read the directions carefully. To answer a multiple-choice question, the directions might tell you to click on the box next to the correct answer. Or they might tell you to click directly on the answer. Click only one answer for each question. Once you are sure you have clicked the right answer, click the Submit button or press the Enter key to move to the next question. In some online tests, you can't go back to a question once you have moved on.

For each question, put a check mark next to the correct answer.

1. What should you do to answer a test question?

____ Click on any answer.

____ Click on the correct answer or answer box.

____ Press the Enter key.

2. How do you go on to the next question?

____ by clicking on an answer

____ by choosing the correct answer

____ by pressing the Enter key or clicking the Submit button

3. How many answers should you choose for each question?

   ___ all of the answers

   ___ two answers

   ___ not more than one answer

4. In how many online tests can you go back and change an answer?

   ___ all

   ___ some

   ___ none

More About Online Tests

The sentences below give more information about how to take an online test.

Marking Answers
- Use the mouse to click on your answers for multiple-choice questions.
- Use the mouse to move answer choices into the fill-in-the-blank boxes.

Giving a Written Response
- To give a written response, type your answer in the space provided.
- Press Enter when you are done with each typed answer.

Moving Through the Test
- Use the toolbar at the top of the page to move around the test.
- Click on the forward button to go forward to new questions.
- Click on the back button to go back to questions you answered earlier. (Some tests allow you to go back to change answers.)

Finishing the Test
- When you have finished the test, click on Submit to show that you are done. You cannot go back once you click on Submit.
- Use the Trash Can button to cancel all of your answers and quit the test. You will have to take the test again later.

Getting Help
- Click the Help button for help.

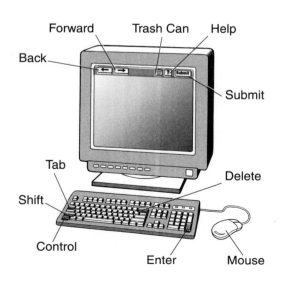

Forward   Trash Can   Help

Back

Submit

Tab

Shift

Control

Enter

Mouse

Delete

Your Turn

Write the number of each item below next to the correct label in the picture.

5. Click here when you are done with the whole test.

6. Press this key at the end of a typed answer.

7. Click here for help.

8. Click here to go back.

9. Click here to cancel the test and try again later.

10. Click here to go forward.

11. Use this to click on multiple-choice answers.

Compare Kinds of Tests

Think about how online tests are like written tests. Think about how they are different. Then write each phrase below in the correct place on the chart.

- check what I know about a subject
- require a pen or pencil
- sometimes don't let me go back and change my answers
- always let me see how many questions I have left
- require a computer
- may ask multiple-choice questions

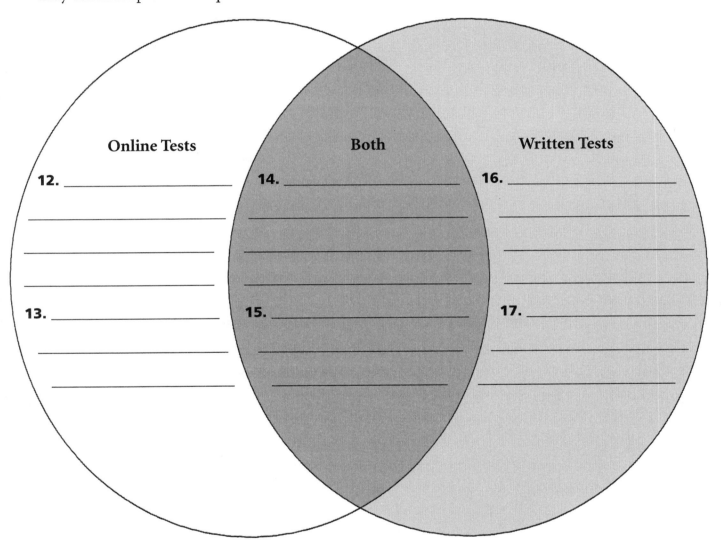

Online Tests

12. _____

_____

_____

_____

13. _____

_____

_____

Both

14. _____

_____

_____

_____

15. _____

_____

_____

Written Tests

16. _____

_____

_____

_____

17. _____

_____

_____

Part A

Before You Take a Test

Answer these questions. Put a check mark next to the correct answer.

1. Should you always study alone?

   ___ yes

   ___ no

2. Will a good night's sleep and a good breakfast help you do better on a test?

   ___ yes

   ___ no

3. Which of these is **not** a good way to get ready for a test?

   ___ Take notes.

   ___ Ask yourself questions.

   ___ Make notes for important words.

   ___ Study all at once.

Read this test situation, then answer the question.

4. You are taking a test that has four sections. You have 40 minutes to finish the test. About how much time should you spend on each section? _____ minutes

As You Take a Test

Part B

Read each set of test directions below. In each set, circle the key words that tell you exactly what to do. Then answer the question.

1. Find the set of words that are nouns. Put a check mark on the line next to the correct set.

   ___ the, these, then   ___ in, on, below

   ___ add, think, write   ___ sentences, lines, circles

2. Find the word that has almost the same meaning as the underlined word. Circle the answer.

   <u>soggy</u>

   sagging   wet

   dry   baggy

3. Fill in the blank with the correct answer. Football is a kind of

   _____.

   helmet   T.V.

   sport   cheer

4. Fill in the circle next to the best answer. If you are unsure of the answer to a test question, you should _____.

   Ⓐ pick the first answer listed

   Ⓑ skip the question and come back to it later

   Ⓒ stop taking the test

   Ⓓ mark more than one answer

5. Draw a line through the answers you know are wrong. Who lives in the White House?

   the White family   the Supreme Court

   the President   George Washington

Part C

Written Responses

Read the writing prompts below. Then put a check mark next to the answer that tells what kind of written response is required.

1. Write a few sentences about your favorite season. Give reasons why you like it.

___ a long narrative response   ___ a short expository response

___ one short sentence   ___ one long story

2. Write a few paragraphs about an important event in your life. Tell why it was important and how it affected you.

___ a long narrative response   ___ a short expository response

___ one or two sentences   ___ a long expository response

Write your own answer to this short writing prompt.

3. Think about your favorite movie. Write a paragraph explaining why you like it.

_____

_____

_____

_____

_____

_____

_____

Read this longer writing prompt. On another sheet of paper, create an outline for your answer. Then write out your answer.

4–5. If you could spend an entire day with a person from the past, whom would you choose? Write a few paragraphs telling why you would choose this person and what the two of you would do during your day together.

Taking Real-World Tests

Part D

Fill in the circle next to the best answer.

1. What does this sign mean?

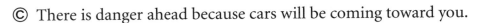

Ⓐ There is a curved road ahead.

Ⓑ You are going against the flow of cars.

Ⓒ There is danger ahead because cars will be coming toward you.

Ⓓ Let other people, cars, or bikes pass before you go ahead.

Put a check mark next to the correct answer.

2. It is OK to tow a friend riding a bike behind your car.
___ true   ___ false

3. You must drive at or below the speed limit.
___ true ___ false

4. How are online tests the same as written tests?

___ Both check what you know about a subject.

___ They don't let you go back and change your answers.

___ Both are taken on computers.

___ Both always let you know how many questions you have left.

5. How are online tests and written tests different?

___ Only written tests ask multiple-choice questions.

___ You use a keyboard and mouse to move through online tests.

___ Only online tests ask fill-in-the-blank questions.

___ You don't need to study for an online test.

TEST TIP

When you are answering questions about a reading passage, read the questions first. That way you'll know what information you need to find. Each time you find an answer to a question, make a light check mark in the margin. When you're done skimming, find the check marks and answer the questions.

LESSON 13   Using an Encyclopedia

Have you ever needed to find information about a topic? You may need to find a quick fact about New York City. Or maybe you need information for a report about whales. One place you can look for facts is an **encyclopedia**.

- An encyclopedia contains articles about many different topics.
- Each article begins with a **heading** that contains a key word, such as **turtles, Texas,** or **tornadoes**. The articles are arranged in alphabetical order.
- An encyclopedia is organized into volumes labeled from A to Z. Each volume contains articles about topics beginning with a certain letter or set of letters.

Topics in an Encyclopedia

Take a look at the set of encyclopedias below. Then answer the questions.

1. In which volume would you find facts about jellyfish? _____

2. In which volume would you find information about volcanoes?

    _____

3. In which volume would you find information about President Abraham Lincoln? _____

4. How many volumes does the letter **c** have? _____

5. What other letter has more than one volume? _____

6. In which volume would you look to find information about spiders?

    _____

Guide Words

Let's say you need to find a fact about spiders. The guide words at the top of the pages can help you find the article on spiders fast.

The guide word on the left page is the first entry on that page. The guide word on the right page is the last entry on that page. To find an entry, look for the guide words that come before and after it in alphabetical order.

KEY WORD

Related article another article linked to a topic

Example

Between which guide words would you find the entry for **spiders**? Circle the correct answer.

space and **spelling**   ⟨**spice** and **spinach**⟩   **stork** and **submarine**

7. Between which guide words would you find the entry for **computers**? Circle the answer.

   circus and **Cleveland**

   cliff dwellings and **Bill Clinton**

   compact disc and **concrete**

8. Between which guide words would you find the entry for **astronaut**? Circle the answer.

   acorn and **adverb**

   apple and **April**

   ash and **Atlanta**

Related Articles

What if the article you find does not contain the information you are looking for? It might direct you to another entry that will help you.

- If an article doesn't have what you're looking for, find the **related articles** listed at the end.
- Related articles are linked to the topic you just read about. You can read a related article by looking in the correct volume.

9. Let's say you want to find facts about bridges in New York City. You look under **New York City** in the encyclopedia, but the article doesn't include what you are looking for. Circle the related articles that are likely to have information you need.

   Hudson River   Subway
   Statue of Liberty   Brooklyn Bridge
   Wall Street   George Washington Bridge

10. Look back at the encyclopedia volumes shown on page 52. In which volumes would you find the related articles you circled? _____

Subheading
a word or phrase that names one of the main ideas in an article, section, or chapter

Parts of an Encyclopedia Article

An encyclopedia article is organized with headings and subheadings. The heading names the topic of the article. The **subheadings** name the main ideas the article covers. Look at the entry about television below. Circle the heading. Underline the subheadings.

Television brings moving pictures and sounds into homes around the world. Since its beginnings in the early 1900s, television has grown to be our most important means of communication.

How it works. Television works by changing light and sound waves into electronic signals. These signals are known as electromagnetic waves. A television set receives these signals. It changes them into the sounds and pictures you see on your TV screen.

Television around the world. Television use varies from place to place. In the United States and Japan, most homes have at least one television. In Africa, there are fewer TVs than in other parts of the world. In the United States, Europe, and Japan, there is a mix of public and private TV stations. In most African countries, the TV stations are run by the government. In China, all TV stations are government owned.

Effects of television. Watching television is a popular activity in many places. Many people say that TV provides viewers with learning opportunities. Viewers can learn about other countries, animals, outer space, and many other topics. However, some say that TV leads to an unrealistic picture of life. Some people also say that the violence on TV could have negative effects on children.

Jobs in television. There are many jobs that have to do with television. On-the-air jobs include acting and reporting the news. There are also technical jobs, such as operating cameras and designing lighting.

Related articles include:

advertising   electronics
radio   videotape recorder

---

11. Which related article would you read if you wanted information about TV commercials?

_____

12. In which encyclopedia volume would you find this related article? (Look at the encyclopedia set shown on page 52.)

_____

13. Which related article would you read if you wanted facts about how to record TV programs?

_____

14. Which subheading would you read first if you were looking for information about television in another country?

_____

Electronic Encyclopedias

There are two kinds of electronic encyclopedias: **CD-ROM** and **online**.

- A **CD-ROM encyclopedia** is a compact disc that has the contents of an encyclopedia on it. To look up articles on your computer, insert the disc and open it. Then search by key word or browse by volume.
- An **online encyclopedia** is located on the Internet.

Here's how to find an online encyclopedia:

Step 1: Use a Web browser on your computer. Type in the name of an encyclopedia you know. If you don't know one, just type in the word **encyclopedias** and click the Search button. Then choose an encyclopedia from the ones that come up on the screen.

Step 2: Once you get to the Web site, there are two ways to find facts. You can search for your topic alphabetically by volume. Or you can enter a key word, such as **monkeys** or **television**. If you enter a key word, the article will appear on the computer screen.

Step 3: With an online encyclopedia, you can often look at the subheadings before reading the article. To read a certain part of an article, just click on the subheading.

Step 4: An online encyclopedia also lists related articles. To read one, click on the link.

KEY WORDS

CD-ROM encyclopedia
an encyclopedia located on a compact disc and accessed through a computer

Online encyclopedia
an encyclopedia located on the Internet and accessed through a Web browser on a computer

Use What You Know

15. Which key word would you use to search for an article describing the weather in Florida?

- Ⓐ southeast
- Ⓑ weather
- Ⓒ sun
- Ⓓ Florida

16. Once you found this article, which subheading would you look for in the article?

- Ⓐ people
- Ⓑ history
- Ⓒ weather
- Ⓓ beaches

17. How do you use an online encyclopedia? Number the steps in the correct order from 1 to 4.

____ **A** If you don't find the facts you need, click on a link to a related article.

____ **B** Do a search for an encyclopedia using a Web browser

____ **C** To find an article, choose a volume or enter a key word.

____ **D** Read the article.

LESSON 14   Using an Almanac and an Atlas

Almanac
a book of facts that is
updated every year

Just the Facts—Almanacs

Where would you look to find out which team won the World Series in 1965? Where can you find what language people speak in Egypt? What will tell you the birthday of your favorite celebrity? An almanac is a book that contains all of this information and much more.

- An **almanac** is a book of facts that is updated every year.
- Almanacs contain news stories and listings of government departments and agencies.
- Almanacs give facts about countries around the world, sports, travel, politics, the arts, and other topics.
- Many almanacs begin with an index.

The text below shows part of an almanac index. Use the index to answer the questions.

State Profiles	431–481	**States, U.S.**	555–589
Alabama	431	Area and Rank	555
Alaska	432	Capitals	561
Arizona	433	Climate	588
Arkansas	434	Education	572
California	435	Famous Natives	557–558
Colorado	436	Governors	578
Connecticut	437	Nicknames and	
Delaware	438	Population	583–586
Florida	439	Public Parks	570
		Tourist Attractions	560–565

1. On what page would you look to find the capital of Montana?

_____

2. Which topic would tell about famous people from your state?

Ⓐ tourist attractions

Ⓑ famous natives

Ⓒ climate

Ⓓ education

3. On what page would you look to find what the winter weather is like in Texas?

_____

4. On what page would you find the state profile for Arizona?

_____

Once you find your topic, go to the page listed in the index. The facts might be organized in a chart. If you looked up **Nicknames and Population,** you might find a chart like this one.

Use the chart to answer the questions below.

U.S. States

State	2002 Population	Nickname
Massachusetts	6,349,097	Bay State, Old Colony
Michigan	9,938,444	Great Lakes State, Wolverine State
Minnesota	4,919,479	North Star State, Gopher State
Mississippi	2,844,658	Magnolia State
Missouri	5,595,211	Show Me State

5. Which state in the chart has the largest population? _____

6. Which state is nicknamed the Show Me State? _____

7. Which state is called the Magnolia State? _____

8. What is the population of Massachusetts? _____

Sometimes information in an almanac is written in sentences or lists. If you looked up California's state profile, you might find this.

State Profile: California

General Facts: With a population of more than 33 million, California ranks as the most populous state. California lies along the western coast. Its landscape includes mountains, valleys, deserts, and forests.

History: American Indians were the first residents of California. The first settlement was a Spanish mission in San Diego. The United States and Mexico fought over California, and the United States finally won the land in 1848. Gold was discovered in California in 1848. This caused thousands of people to flock to California in the "Gold Rush."

Capital: Sacramento
Motto: Eureka (I have found it!)
Flower: golden poppy

Bird: California valley quail
Tree: California redwood
Song: "I Love You, California"

STRATEGY TIP

When you read charts, look at the headings to make sure you understand what the chart is showing. Headings can appear at the top of a chart, down the side of it, or both.

Atlas
a book of maps

Latitude
how far north or south of the equator a place is

Longitude
how far east or west a place is from the prime meridian

Use the state profile information to answer these questions.

9. What does California's state motto mean?

Ⓐ the Gold Rush

Ⓑ "I Love You, California"

Ⓒ golden poppy

Ⓓ I have found it!

10. How many people live in California?

Ⓐ 10

Ⓑ 3 million

Ⓒ 33 million

Ⓓ 20 thousand

11. What is California's state flower?

Ⓐ California valley quail

Ⓑ golden poppy

Ⓒ petunia

Ⓓ redwood blossom

12. When did settlers first find gold?

Ⓐ 1848

Ⓑ 1985

Ⓒ 1829

Ⓓ 1900

Maps and More Maps—Atlases

An **atlas** is a book of maps. An atlas often contains other kinds of information too. There are many types of atlases and maps. For example, there are world atlases, atlases of the oceans, and road atlases.

At the back of an atlas, there is an index. The index lists in alphabetical order the places that the atlas shows. It also lists the page number where you can find information about each place. The **latitude** and **longitude** numbers tell exactly where each place is located on the globe.

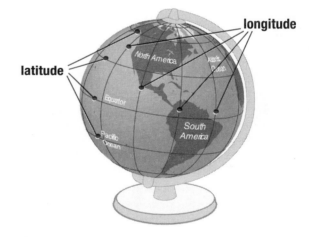

This text shows part of an index from an atlas of the United States.

Name	Page	Latitude	Longitude
Atlanta, GA	104	33.45°N	84.23°W
Boston, MA	212	42.21°N	71.04°W
Chicago, IL	301	41.53°N	87.38°W
Dallas, TX	340	32.45°N	96.48°W

Use the atlas index on page 58 to answer these questions.

13. On what page would you find a map of Chicago?

_____

15. On what page would you find a map of Atlanta?

_____

14. Fill in the latitude and longitude of Dallas, Texas.

Latitude _____

Longitude _____

16. Fill in the latitude and longitude of Boston, Massachusetts.

Latitude _____

Longitude _____

Look at the two maps below. Read the titles to find out what each map shows.

Major Rivers of the West

Some Time Zones

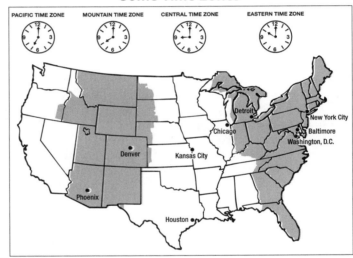

Use the maps to answer these questions.

17. Put a check mark next to the map you would use to find out what time zone Chicago is in.

18. Into which body of water does the Colorado River empty?

Ⓐ Gulf of California

Ⓑ Gulf of Mexico

Ⓒ Atlantic Ocean

Ⓓ Arkansas River

19. Put a star by the map you would look at to find where the Rio Grande is located.

20. Which two cities are in the same time zone?

Ⓐ Denver and Houston

Ⓑ Phoenix and Chicago

Ⓒ Detroit and New York City

Ⓓ Baltimore and Kansas City

Using the Library

Fiction
stories about events that did not really happen

Periodical
a publication issued on a regular schedule, such as a magazine

Reference book
a book with useful information that has been carefully organized

Dewey decimal system
a library organizing system that puts books into categories by topic

Where can you go to study, flip through the latest magazines, surf the Internet, and do research for a project? The answer is the library. Libraries keep books (both **fiction** and **nonfiction**), newspapers, magazines (also called **periodicals**), and **reference books** for people to read and borrow. A library is a great place, once you figure out how to use it.

The Basics

When you first go into a library, there is usually an information desk. The librarian who sits there can answer your questions. There are computers set up to help you find books. You can check out books from the library, which means that you can borrow them for a certain period of time. If you don't return the book on time, you have to pay a fine. A library card is needed to check out a book. You can apply for one at the front desk.

Most libraries are organized using a system called the **Dewey decimal system**. This system puts books into categories by topic. The basic Dewey decimal categories are listed below. Each topic has a number series. That way, books about the same topic are all in the same place. For example, all religion books are shelved together in the 200 category. Each religion book is given a call number starting with 2 (like 257.92).

Draw a line to match each sample book with the category it can be found in. (Hint: Match the reference call number under each book to a Dewey decimal category.) The first one has been done for you.

Sample Books

1. *Poems about New York City,* by Todd Dunn, Ref. 812.45

2. *How Plants Grow,* by Ella Green, Ref. 559.21

3. *The Life of Babe Ruth,* by Bobby Hall, Ref. 931.84

Dewey Decimal Category	Topic
000	General Information: Reference Books, Periodicals, News Media
100	Philosophy and Psychology
200	Religion
300	Social Sciences
400	Language
500	Natural Science and Math
600	Applied Science and Technology
700	The Arts: Music, Sports, Dance
800	Literature
900	Geography, Biography, History

You can check out books in many of these categories. You usually cannot check out reference books or current periodicals, however. You can read these at the library. You can also make copies of any pages that you need.

Show What You Know

Answer these questions by filling in the circle next to the correct answer.

4. In which section could you find a biography about jazz musician Miles Davis?

   Ⓐ 100 Philosophy and Psychology

   Ⓑ 400 Language

   Ⓒ 700 The Arts

   Ⓓ 900 Geography, Biography, History

5. In which section could you find the newspaper headlines from the day you were born?

   Ⓐ 000 General Information: News Media

   Ⓑ 300 Social Sciences

   Ⓒ 400 Language

   Ⓓ 800 Literature

6. In which section could you find poems by your favorite author?

   Ⓐ 100 Philosophy and Psychology

   Ⓑ 700 The Arts

   Ⓒ 800 Literature

   Ⓓ 900 Geography, Biography, History

7. In which section could you find a book about insects?

   Ⓐ 200 Religion

   Ⓑ 300 Social Sciences

   Ⓒ 500 Natural Science and Math

   Ⓓ 800 Literature

STUDY TIP

Fiction is often a separate category from literature. Instead of being classified with Dewey decimal numbers, fiction books may be classified with the letter F and then alphabetized by the author's last name.

Other Resources

In addition to books, the library has other materials that you can use and enjoy.

- You can read old issues of newspapers on microfilm.
- You can check out videos and sometimes watch videos in the media center.
- You can listen to and check out books on tape, as well as tapes that can help you learn another language.
- Most libraries have a computer center you can use. Some computers are reserved for the library database, which is how you find books. Often there are other computers with Internet access. Some libraries have computer labs where you can type and print reports.
- You can use copy machines.

Library Treasure Hunt

You have been invited to a Day of the Dead party. You know that this is a Mexican holiday, but you don't know much else. Time to hit the books! Look at the library map below.

Now go on a treasure hunt to locate items 8 to 13 on the map. Put a star on the map next to each place you locate. Then draw a line to the next place.

8. First find an encyclopedia article that gives the basic facts. You could look up **Day of the Dead**. If that doesn't work, try **Mexico**.

9. Next, find a book about the history of Mexico.

10. You find out that on the Day of the Dead, people celebrate their loved ones who are no longer alive. You want to know more about what people do at the celebration. Find a book about Mexican culture and holidays. (Hint: You might find this in the social sciences section.)

11. You find out that on this holiday, people eat candy skulls. They make displays full of flowers, fruit, and photos of their loved ones. You want to find pictures of the displays so you'll know what to expect. Find a magazine article about how the Day of the Dead is celebrated in Mexico today.

12. You want to read a short story by Mexican-American author Gary Soto before you go to the party. Find a book of stories written by him.

13. Check out the books at the front desk. Have fun at the party!

LESSON 16   Using the Library Database

You can search for a book in the library's database. There are two types of databases: **electronic databases** and **card catalogs**. Electronic databases are used at most libraries today, but some libraries use a card catalog.

Electronic Databases

You use an electronic database on the computer. Most libraries have computers reserved for people who need to use the database. You will find a screen that looks something like this one. It will tell you how to begin your search.

There are four main ways to search the database.

By author: If you know the author's name, type it into the search box. Always enter the author's last name and then the first name. The search will find all the books by that author.

By title: If you know the title of the book you want, enter that into the search box. The search will find all books with that title.

By subject: If you want a book about a certain subject, but you don't know any titles or authors, search by subject or topic. If you enter a big topic, you may be given some smaller topics to pick from. For example, if you search for **sports,** you will be shown more specific topics, such as **water sports, ball games,** or **extreme sports.**

By key words: If you only know a few words from a book title, use a key word search. A key word search will list every book with those words in the title. You must sort through the titles to find the book you want.

KEY WORDS

Electronic database a large collection of online information about library resources that is organized for rapid search and retrieval

Card catalog a manual way of organizing information about books in a library

Public Library

| HOME | DATABASE | MY ACCOUNT | HELP |

Select a search option:
◯ Author   ◯ Title   ◉ Subject   ◯ Key Words

Please enter a word or phrase:

| SEARCH |

1. Which type of search would you use to find a book by the author Sandra Cisneros?

   Ⓐ subject

   Ⓑ title

   Ⓒ author

   Ⓓ key words

2. Which type of search would you use to find a book about sports in Japan?

   Ⓐ subject

   Ⓑ title

   Ⓒ author

   Ⓓ key words

Parts of a Database Chart

If you searched for the book *Mexican Holidays* by Ana Cortes, you might find a chart like this:

Location	Call Number	Volume	Material	Status
Main: Floor 3	394.29		Hardback	On Shelf
Downtown Branch	394.29		Paperback	Borrowed

Location: If the book is at the library you are searching from, this tells you in what floor or room to find it. If the book is at another library, it tells you which library to go to.

Call number: This tells you the book's classification number in the Dewey decimal system. The number lets you know which section of the library to find the book in.

Volume: If the book is part of a multivolume set, this column tells you which volume to look for.

Material: This tells you whether the entry is a hardback or paperback book, or an audiovisual or musical recording.

Status: This tells you whether the book is on the shelf, borrowed (checked out), or missing.

Answer the following questions.

3. What is the call number for the book *Mexican Holidays*? _____

4. In which two locations can you find the book? _____
   and _____

5. Will you be able to check out the book at the downtown branch?

   ____ yes ____ no

Card Catalogs

If your library uses a card catalog, there are three ways to search for a book: by author, by title, and by subject. The card catalog is organized in alphabetical order. Each card contains the title, author, publisher, date, and call number of one library book or recording.

6. Which way of searching can be done in a computer database but not in a card catalog?

   Ⓐ subject   Ⓒ author

   Ⓑ title   Ⓓ key words

LESSON 17　Finding Facts on the Internet

Where do you go when you want to find a fact—fast? The Internet can be a source of quick information about almost any topic. Follow these steps to do a Web search:

Step 1: Locate a **search engine** on your Web browser.

Step 2: Think of a key word or phrase that will lead you to the information you need. Then type this in the search box.

Step 3: Click on the Search button. You will see a list of links that are related to your key word.

Step 4: Read the search results. Click on any link that looks helpful. This will take you to a Web site.

Picking the Right Key Word

You might have to try using three or four key words before you find the information you need. Usually the most specific key words get the best results.

| Example | What would be the best key word to enter if you wanted information about Stonehenge, in England? |

England　　　　　　　　Stonehenge

rock structures　　　　　travel

Stonehenge would be the best key word because it will lead you to sites just about that place. **England, rock structures,** and **travel** are too general.

Fill in the circle next to the correct answer.

1. What's the best key word for information about travel in Australia?
   - Ⓐ Sydney
   - Ⓒ travel
   - Ⓑ kangaroos
   - Ⓓ Australia

2. What's the best key word for information about poetry slams?
   - Ⓐ slam dunk
   - Ⓒ celebrity poets
   - Ⓑ poetry slam
   - Ⓓ rhymes

KEY WORD

Search engine
a Web site that helps you search for information on the Internet through the use of key words

TECH TIP

There are two ways to get information on the Internet. You can do a key word search using a search engine. Or you can type the name of a Web site in the search box.

More Practice with Key Words

Finding the right key word usually takes trial and error. If you need to find a fact, you might have to try several searches.

Write the key word you would use first to find these facts.

3. How tall is Mount McKinley, in Alaska?

_____

4. In what South American country would you find the Nazca lines?

_____

Now do a search on the Internet using the key words you chose for questions 3 and 4. If you find the fact you need with your key word, put a check mark next to the question. If you have to try another key word, write your second key word after the first one.

Using Two Key Words

One way to make a search more specific is to use two key words.

5. Say you want to find information about sports camps. You search using the key word **sports**. You get 605 search results! Which of these words could be a second key word to help you narrow your search?

Ⓐ camp   Ⓒ game

Ⓑ tent   Ⓓ score

6. What if you want information about keeping a king snake as a pet? Which key words would you use?

Ⓐ **snakes** and **reptiles**   Ⓒ **crazy** and **snake**

Ⓑ **king snakes** and **pets**   Ⓓ **pets** and **animals**

Checking the Facts

The Internet has some information posted by official sources, such as government agencies and encyclopedia publishers. It also contains information posted by many individuals and groups. There are so many sources of information on the Internet that it can be hard to know which ones to trust. It's best to check the accuracy of the facts you find on the Internet by looking at a second source. If you can, check the facts you find on the Internet against an encyclopedia or another printed source.

READING TIP

Many Internet sites have pages that are cluttered with pictures, boxes, and headlines. This can make the pages hard to read. Try not to let the clutter distract you. Focus only on finding and reading the information you need.

LESSON 18   Choosing the Right Reference Source

By now you know the facts about all kinds of reference sources. The trick is knowing when to use them! Think about it: if you wanted to find out about the eating habits of bears, you certainly wouldn't look in an atlas. You'd probably find the best information in an encyclopedia. And if you wanted to know how late your local art museum is open, you wouldn't check an almanac. Your best bet would be to look on the Internet.

Different Sources for Different Purposes

Here's a quick review of what information each reference source contains.

- An **encyclopedia** contains short articles about general topics.
- An **almanac** is a book of facts that is updated every year. It has news stories and facts from each year, plus information about sports, travel, the arts, and politics.
- An **atlas** is a book of maps. Types of atlases include a world atlas, a road atlas, and an atlas of the oceans.
- The **library** contains books, reference books, newspapers, magazines, and audiovisual materials.
- The **Internet** has Web sites with information about almost any topic.

Use the information on reference sources to answer these questions.

1. Which source would you use if you wanted to find out which country won the most gold medals at the 2000 Summer Olympic Games?

   _____

2. Which source would you use if you wanted to find out the show times at your local movie theater?

   _____

3. Which source would you use if you needed to look at a detailed map of Florida?

   _____

4. Where would you go if you needed a book and a magazine article about hurricanes?

   _____

5. Which source would you use if you needed facts for a short report about cheetahs?

   _____

6. Which source would you use if you wanted to find out how many tourists visit the United States each year?

   _____

> **THINK ABOUT IT**
>
> The information you find on the Internet can't always be trusted. When you visit a Web site, ask yourself: Who has posted this information? Can this source be trusted?

Show What You Know

All of these reference sources can be found at the library.

Answer the questions below by using this library map. Remember to choose the right reference source!

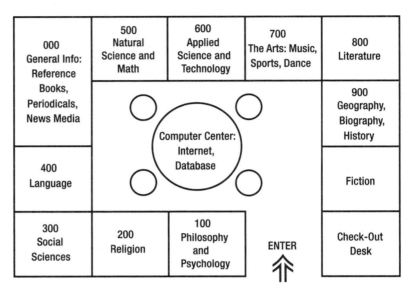

7. Place a star by the spot where you could find a chart with information about the high and low temperatures of U.S. cities. Write your reference source here. _____

8. Put a check mark next to the spot where you could find the score of yesterday's football game. Write your reference source here.

_____

9. Draw a circle around the resource that could help you find out if a particular book is already checked out.

10. Place an X by the spot where you could find a map of the streets of Paris, France. Write your reference source here. _____

11. If you wanted to find a novel about Paris just for fun, in which section would you look? _____

12. Draw a box around the resource that could help you find a Web site with facts about traveling to China.

13. Draw a triangle by the spot where you could look up the birthdate of the inventor Thomas Edison. Write your reference source here.

_____

14. If you wanted to read a biography about Thomas Edison, in which section would you look? _____

What Do You Think?

Take a look at these letters. They were written by students seeking advice about reference sources. After each question, write your advice. Tell the students which reference sources they should use. Try to give each student at least two suggestions.

Hey!

I need to write a report about fashion styles of the 1960s and 70s. Right now my only reference source is old photos of my mom and dad wearing bell-bottom jeans! I have no idea where to start looking. Where do you think I can find this information?

Sincerely,

Clueless

15. Dear Clueless, _____

_____

_____

_____

_____

_____

_____

Greetings! I am writing a speech for my debate class. My topic is how cars have changed life in America. I need some basic facts about cars. I need some statistics about how many people own cars. I could also use some maps to show how many highways there are in the U.S. Where should I look for this information? Thanks!

Sincerely,

The Car Guy

16. Dear Car Guy, _____

_____

_____

_____

_____

_____

_____

Part A   Using Encyclopedias, Almanacs, and Atlases

Look at the set of encyclopedias. Then answer the questions below.

1. In which volume would you find facts about lizards?

   _____

2. In which volume would you find facts about Martin Luther King, Jr.? _____

3. Between which guide words would you find the entry for **earthquake**? Circle one pair.

   ear and **Ecuador**

   Egypt and **Albert Einstein**

   electricity and **English**

Look back at the atlas index on page 58. Then answer these questions.

4. On what page would you find a map showing the location of Dallas, Texas? _____

5. On what page would you find a map showing the location of Boston, Massachusetts?

   _____

Look back at the almanac index on page 56 to help you answer these questions.

6. On what page could you find the state profile for Delaware?

   _____

7. On what page could you find out what public parks are in your state? _____

8. Which topic would you look up if you wanted to find out what interesting sites you could visit in Kansas?

   Ⓐ climate

   Ⓑ public parks

   Ⓒ tourist attractions

   Ⓓ famous natives

Look at the chart. Then answer the questions below.

U.S. States

State	2002 Population	Nickname
Massachusetts	6,349,097	Bay State, Old Colony
Michigan	9,938,444	Great Lakes State, Wolverine State
Minnesota	4,919,479	North Star State, Gopher State
Mississippi	2,844,658	Magnolia State
Missouri	5,595,211	Show Me State

9. The Wolverine State is one of two nicknames for which state?

Ⓐ Mississippi   Ⓒ Michigan

Ⓑ Minnesota   Ⓓ Missouri

10. What is the population of Missouri? _____

Using the Library and Its Database   # Part B

Use the Dewey decimal chart on page 60 to answer these questions.

1. In which library section could you find a book about modern art?

Ⓐ 300 Social Sciences

Ⓑ 700 The Arts

Ⓒ 800 Literature

2. If you need to take home information from a current magazine issue, what should you do?

Ⓐ look in a different reference source

Ⓑ make a photocopy of it

Ⓒ go to another library

3. In which library section could you find a book that would help you learn Spanish?

Ⓐ 400 Language

Ⓑ 200 Religion

Ⓒ 900 Geography, Biography, History

4. Which of these things can't you do at a library?

Ⓐ read old copies of newspapers

Ⓑ check out books on tape

Ⓒ listen to the radio

Ⓓ use the copy machines

TEST TIP

When answering multiple-choice questions, remember to eliminate wrong answers first.

Complete the following sentences about using a library database.

5. If you know a few words from a book title, but not the whole title, you should search by

_____.

6. Fill in the correct circle. A book's call number tells you

_____.

Ⓐ in which library section you can find it

Ⓑ how to order it by telephone

Ⓒ how many copies exist

7. If you know the name of the person who wrote a book, you should search by

_____.

8. Fill in the correct circle. If a book's status is "borrowed," that means _____.

Ⓐ you can still check it out

Ⓑ someone else has checked it out

Ⓒ it is lost

Part C Finding Information on the Internet

Answer the following questions about using a search engine.

1. Which of these statements about searching the Internet is false?

Ⓐ A search will provide you with links.

Ⓑ You don't need to check another source.

Ⓒ Specific key words are better than general ones.

Ⓓ You can find plenty of facts.

2. What's the best key word to use for facts about the Liberty Bell?

Ⓐ Philadelphia   Ⓒ Liberty Bell

Ⓑ historic things   Ⓓ famous bells

3. What two key words would you choose if you wanted to find a recipe for gnocchi, an Italian dish?

_____ and _____

4. What two key words or phrases would you use if you wanted to find out who the president of South Africa is?

_____ and _____

Choosing the Right Reference Source

Part D

Answer the following questions about reference sources.

1. Which source would you use if you wanted to find out which musicians won Grammy Awards in 1995?

_____

2. Which source would you use if you wanted to find basic facts about the sport called cricket?

_____

3. Which source would you use if you wanted to find an online encyclopedia?

_____

4. Which source would you use if you wanted to find a map of the streets in the city of Istanbul, Turkey?

_____

Read this letter by a student asking for advice on reference sources. Give the student your advice on the lines below.

Hello! I am working on a project about movies. I need to find out some basic facts about filmmaking and the history of movies. I also need a list of the most popular movies of the 1990s. Oh, and a biography of a famous movie star would be great. Help! I don't know where to look.

Thanks!

Movie Lover

5. Dear Movie Lover,_____

_____

_____

_____

_____

_____

_____

TEST TIP

When you finish a test, take time to look it over again. Make sure you answered every question. Try it now! Look back over this practice test. Did you complete every item?

LESSON 19   Understanding Textbook Features

KEY WORDS

Key term
an important word or phrase that is explained in a chapter

Focus question
a question at the beginning of a chapter in a book that helps set a purpose for reading

Caption
words located next to a picture that tell what the picture shows

Graphic aid
something that gives information in a visual way

Textbooks give information that students are responsible for learning. These books have special parts that can make new topics easier to understand. Knowing the purpose of each part can help you understand your textbooks.

- The title of a chapter tells what the chapter is about.
- Headings and subheadings tell what each section of a chapter is about.
- Many textbook chapters have a list of **key terms** at the beginning. These name important concepts that are discussed in the chapter. In many textbooks, a glossary at the back of the book gives a definition for each term.
- In some textbooks, each chapter begins with a **focus question**. This question can help you set a purpose for reading.
- Most textbooks have photographs and drawings that illustrate important concepts. **Captions** next to these pictures tell what the pictures show.
- Graphs, time lines, and other **graphic aids** give information about numbers or time periods in a visual way.

Get Ready to Read

Look at the textbook passage on the next page. Then follow these directions.

1. Put a star next to the focus question. Write what you think this passage is about.

_____

2. Underline the title of the passage. Circle the headings.

3. The topic of this passage may be new to you. Fill in the circle next to the strategy that can help you understand it.

Ⓐ skip the hard parts

Ⓑ read as fast as you can

Ⓒ read fairly slowly

STRATEGY TIP

Read at the right speed! When you read about a topic that's familiar to you, it's fine to read more quickly. When you read about a topic that is new to you, slow down! It takes more time to read long sentences and new words.

Read a Textbook Passage

Now read the passage. Then answer the questions on the next page.

Supersonic Air Travel

The Search for Speed. In the early 1940s, scientists worked to develop supersonic planes—planes that could fly faster than the speed of sound. Early attempts to reach this speed failed. The planes were ripped apart by shock waves. Then in 1947, U.S. Air Force Captain Charles E. Yeager flew an X-1 rocket plane. It went faster than the speed of sound. During the next 20 years, several countries built supersonic war planes. But some scientists dreamed of building a different kind of speedy plane. They wanted to build an SST, a supersonic transport plane built to carry passengers.

The Concorde. In 1962 Britain and France agreed to work together to build an SST plane. The plane they built, a jet called the Concorde, made its first flight in 1969. It began carrying passengers in 1976. This jet can fly at speeds up to 1,350 miles per hour. That is more than twice the speed of regular passenger jets. A flight from New York to London can take about 3 hours and 40 minutes. A regular jet makes the same trip in about 8 hours.

Problems with SSTs. Not everyone loves the Concorde. Some people say it is a costly, noisy, and limited way to travel. The jet burns much more fuel than regular jets do. That is one reason a New York-London round-trip ticket can cost $12,000. The jet's engines are very loud too. As the jet passes the speed of sound, it causes a sonic boom* that is strong enough to break windows. For this reason, SSTs fly mainly over water and to very few places.

* As a jet passes the speed of sound, it pushes air forward in a cone-shaped shock wave. This causes a loud sound called a *sonic boom.*

Focus Question

What are the benefits and costs of supersonic air travel?

Key Terms

**speed of sound
supersonic transport
passenger
sonic boom**

The Concorde flies smoothly above all weather at 60,000 feet above the earth.

4. What does **supersonic** mean?

    Ⓐ really loud   Ⓒ faster than the speed of light

    Ⓑ faster than the speed of sound   Ⓓ too fast to be seen

5. Who flew the first supersonic plane?

_____

6. What is good about supersonic travel?

    Ⓐ It's quiet.   Ⓒ It's fast.

    Ⓑ It's cheap.   Ⓓ It burns less fuel.

7–8. What are two problems with SST passenger planes?

_____

_____

9. About how long is a flight from New York to London on the Concorde?

    Ⓐ 9 hours   Ⓒ 7 hours

    Ⓑ $3\frac{1}{2}$ hours   Ⓓ $5\frac{1}{2}$ hours

10. Draw a circle around the part of the passage that explains what the term **sonic boom** means.

11. What information does the photo caption provide?

    Ⓐ how fast the SST plane flies   Ⓒ what cities the SST plane flies to

    Ⓑ how high the SST plane flies   Ⓓ where the first SST plane was built

12. Did you read this passage quickly or slowly? Why?

_____

_____

_____

LESSON 20   Using Titles and Pictures to Predict Content

To **preview** means to look ahead. When you preview a textbook chapter, you look for clues that help **predict** what it will be about. Let's say you open a chapter of a history book. You see pictures of families with all their belongings. From these clues, you predict that the chapter will talk about migration—people moving from one region to another.

To preview a chapter, follow these steps:

Step 1: Read the **title**. It tells what the chapter is about. Read the **headings** and **subheadings**. They will give more clues. Look for **key words** to help you predict what the chapter will say about its topic.

Step 2: Look at the **photographs** and **drawings**. See if you can refine your prediction.

Step 3: Read the **captions**. They can help you understand what the pictures show.

Preview and Predict

Follow the steps above to preview the passage on the next page. (Don't read it yet.) Then answer these questions.

1. What do you predict this passage is about?

   _____

   _____

   _____

2. What helped you make your prediction? (You may mark more than one answer.)

   Ⓐ the title

   Ⓑ the headings

   Ⓒ the picture

   Ⓓ the caption

3. Based on the headings, the picture, and the caption, refine your prediction about the passage. Now what do you think the passage is about?

   _____

   _____

   _____

4. What is one thing you predict you will learn from this passage?

   _____

   _____

Read and Check Your Predictions

Now read the passage. Then answer the questions that follow.

Linking the Coasts

The Need for a Coast-to-Coast Railroad. In 1860, how could you travel from New York to San Francisco? At the time, there were a few ways to do it. However, none of them were fast. You could travel by boat. But the boat had to travel all the way around South America. You could travel by train to the Midwest and then join a wagon train. But the entire trip could take up to six months. Traveling by foot took even longer than that.

The Rails Stretch Westward. By 1860 there were 30,000 miles of railroad lines in the United States. However, none connected the East Coast with the West Coast. Many people wanted a coast-to-coast railroad, especially those living in California after the Gold Rush. In 1862 President Lincoln signed a law called the Pacific Railroad Act. It promised to help pay for a railroad to the West Coast. The railroad would cross 2,000 miles of western plains, deserts, and mountains. Soon crews were busy laying track. America's first coast-to-coast railroad was born.

In 1860, the farthest west a railroad traveler could go was St. Joseph, Missouri.

5. Were your predictions about the passage correct? ___ yes ___ no

If not, look back at the clues you used. Think about how you might have used them to make a different prediction.

6. What is this passage mostly about?

Ⓐ how to take a boat around South America

Ⓑ laws signed by President Lincoln

Ⓒ the beginnings of a railroad across the United States

Ⓓ the California Gold Rush

Make Another Prediction

Take a look at the heading, pictures, and captions of the passage on the next page. Answer the questions below.

7. What do you think the passage will be about? _____

_____

8. Name one thing you predict that you will learn from this passage.

_____

Two Railroads Race to the Finish. The builders of the first railroad to go from coast to coast had a plan. Two railroads would start from opposite points and meet in the middle. The Central Pacific Railroad began at Sacramento, California. It worked east. The Union Pacific Railroad began at Omaha, Nebraska. It worked west. The Central Pacific workers faced the tough job of laying track through the Sierra Nevada mountains. Blasting tunnels through mountains, workers often gained only inches a day. Work went faster for the Union Pacific workers. On May 10, 1869, the two railroads met at Promontory Point, Utah. A hammer drove in the last spike, a golden one. The news flashed across telegraph lines. The coast-to-coast railroad was complete! Now people could cross the West in about six days.

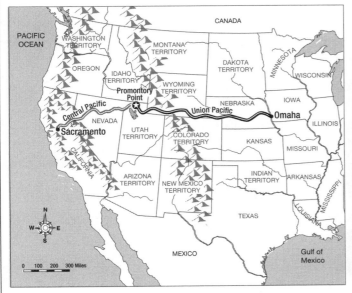

More than 20,000 workers helped build the two railroads. Most of the workers were Chinese or Irish.

The two railroads were joined at Promontory Point, Utah Territory.

Now read the passage and answer these questions.

9. Was your prediction about the passage correct? ____ yes ____ no

If not, look back at the clues you used. Think about how you might have used them to make a different prediction.

10. What is this passage mainly about?

   Ⓐ the Sierra Nevada mountains

   Ⓑ the golden spike

   Ⓒ Sacramento, California

   Ⓓ the construction of a coast-to-coast railroad

11. Where did the two railroads meet? _____

12. Why did the work of the Union Pacific Railroad go more quickly?

_____

_____

THINK ABOUT IT

Do you think the plan of having two companies race to build the railroad was a good idea? Why or why not?

LESSON 21   Interpreting Graphic Aids

KEY WORDS

Time line
a graphic aid that shows events in time order on a line

Bar graph
a graph with bars that represent numbers

You've probably heard the old saying, "A picture is worth a thousand words." Pictures and other kinds of graphic aids help readers see and understand what words tell about. That is why most textbooks are filled with photographs, drawings, maps, charts, time lines, and graphs.

Reading Time Lines

A **time line** organizes events that happened over a period of time in a way that is easy to see. It lists events in the order in which they occurred. Here are some tips for reading and understanding a time line.

- Read the **title** first. This names the topic of the time line.
- Look at the first and last **dates** to find the time period covered.
- As you read, remember that you can determine the number of years between two events by looking at the date when each event occurred and figuring out the difference.

Look at the time line. Then answer the questions.

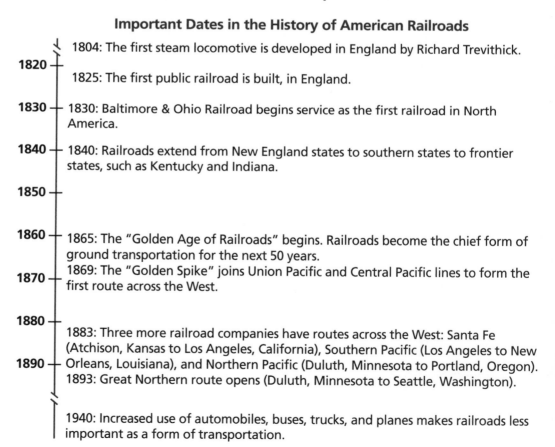

Important Dates in the History of American Railroads

1804: The first steam locomotive is developed in England by Richard Trevithick.

1820

1825: The first public railroad is built, in England.

1830

1830: Baltimore & Ohio Railroad begins service as the first railroad in North America.

1840

1840: Railroads extend from New England states to southern states to frontier states, such as Kentucky and Indiana.

1850

1860

1865: The "Golden Age of Railroads" begins. Railroads become the chief form of ground transportation for the next 50 years.

1870

1869: The "Golden Spike" joins Union Pacific and Central Pacific lines to form the first route across the West.

1880

1883: Three more railroad companies have routes across the West: Santa Fe (Atchison, Kansas to Los Angeles, California), Southern Pacific (Los Angeles to New Orleans, Louisiana), and Northern Pacific (Duluth, Minnesota to Portland, Oregon).

1890

1893: Great Northern route opens (Duluth, Minnesota to Seattle, Washington).

1940: Increased use of automobiles, buses, trucks, and planes makes railroads less important as a form of transportation.

1. What is the topic of this time line?_____

_____

2. How many years are there between the first event and the last event in the time line?

(A) 100 (C) 136

(B) 25 (D) 98

3. When did the "Golden Age of Railroads" begin? _____

4. Put these events in order from first to last. Write the numbers 1 to 4 on the lines.

_____ **A** Great Northern route opens.

_____ **B** First steam locomotive is built.

_____ **C** Baltimore & Ohio Railroad begins.

_____ **D** First route across the West is completed.

Reading Bar Graphs

A **bar graph** uses bars to present numbers in a visual way. Bar graphs help you understand and compare numbers. Here are some tips for reading a bar graph:

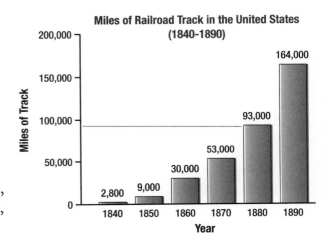

- Read the **title** first. Identify the topic of the bar graph.
- Next, read the **headings** across the bottom and along the left side. Each heading explains the information that is plotted on that side of the graph.
- To read the graph, follow each bar to its highest point. Then look to the number scale at the left. For example, look at the graph at the right. You will see that in 1880, there were about 93,000 miles of railroad track.

Look at the bar graph. Then answer the questions.

5. What does the bar graph show?

(A) train cars in the 1800s

(B) workers on the railroad

(C) miles of track in the United States

(D) train passengers in the 1800s

6. What time period does the graph cover?

(A) 1840–1850

(B) 1840–1890

(C) 1804–1940

(D) 1840–1940

7. About how many miles of track were there in 1870?

(A) 2,000

(C) 53,000

(B) 30,000

(D) 93,000

8. Between which two years was the greatest increase in the amount of track?

(A) 1840–1850

(B) 1850–1860

(C) 1870–1880

(D) 1880–1890

Reading Pie Charts

A **pie chart** is a picture that shows the parts that make up a whole. You can think of it like a pizza cut into slices of different sizes. Each slice represents a percentage or fraction of the whole pie. All of the pieces together stand for 100%. As with a bar graph, the first thing to do when you come across a pie chart is to read the title. It tells you what the chart is measuring. You can get most of the information you need just by looking at the chart.

Look at the pie chart. Then answer the questions below.

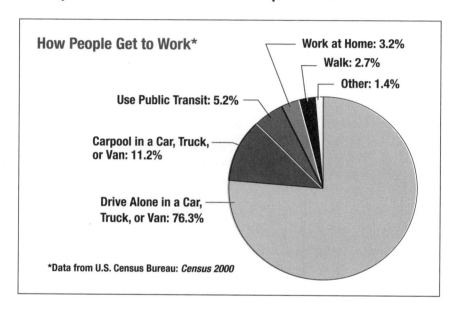

How People Get to Work*

- Work at Home: 3.2%
- Walk: 2.7%
- Other: 1.4%
- Use Public Transit: 5.2%
- Carpool in a Car, Truck, or Van: 11.2%
- Drive Alone in a Car, Truck, or Van: 76.3%

*Data from U.S. Census Bureau: *Census 2000*

9. How many ways of getting to work are shown in this chart?

_____

10. What is the most common way of getting to work?

_____

11. What percentage of people drive to work in a carpool?

_____

12. Do more people use public transportation or walk to work?

_____

WRITING TIP

Whenever possible, use complete sentences when writing answers to questions. You can do this by turning the question into a sentence that includes your answer. For example, the question "What is the most common way of getting to work?" becomes "The most common way of getting to work is _____."

LESSON 22   Interpreting Maps and Globes

Have you ever made a wrong turn in a new city and become completely lost? If this has happened to you, you know how important it is to be able to read a map.

- A **map** is a drawing that shows where different places are in relation to each other.
- A **globe** is a map of the world that is in the shape of planet Earth. A globe helps you see where all the places in the world are in relation to each other.

Using Map Parts

There are many different kinds of maps. Each kind of map gives different information about an area. Most maps have these parts: a legend, a scale, and a compass rose.

A **legend** has little pictures called symbols. The symbols stand for information on the map. A **scale of miles** shows you how much an inch of space on the map stands for in miles. The scale is marked like a ruler. A **compass rose** shows the four main directions and sometimes the directions in between.

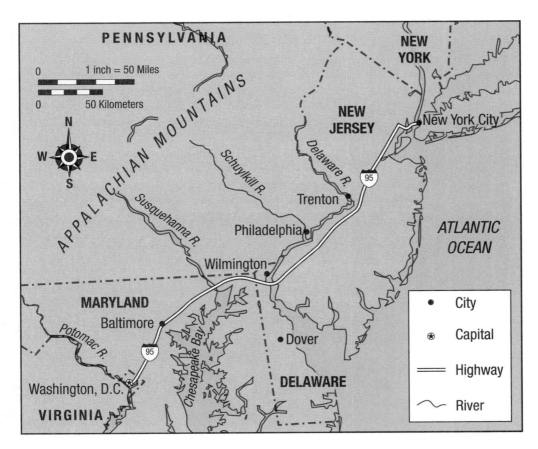

KEY WORDS

Map
a drawing that shows the locations of places in an area

Globe
a map of the world that is in the shape of planet Earth

Legend
a list of symbols that stand for information on a map

Scale of miles
a drawing that shows how much an inch of space on a map stands for in miles

Compass rose
a drawing that shows the four main directions on a map

Study the map on page 83. Then answer these questions.

1. What is the direction of travel from New York City to Philadelphia?

    Ⓐ northeast   Ⓒ northwest

    Ⓑ southeast   Ⓓ southwest

2. What mountain range is west of Trenton? _____

3. On this map, how many miles does one inch stand for? _____

4. About how many miles is Baltimore from Washington, D.C.? _____

Reading Road Maps

A road map shows the roads and highways that connect communities. It also gives other information, such as the locations of parks, airports, rivers, highway rest stops, and campgrounds.

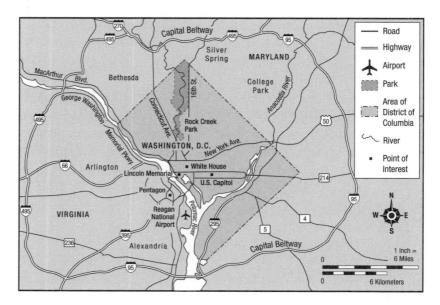

Use the road map to answer these questions.

5. Which road forms a circle around Washington, D.C.?

    Ⓐ Highway 395

    Ⓑ Capital Beltway

    Ⓒ Highway 295

    Ⓓ MacArthur Boulevard

6. What river runs past the Lincoln Memorial? _____

7. Find Rock Creek Park. Which part of Washington, D.C., is it in?

    Ⓐ north   Ⓒ south

    Ⓑ east   Ⓓ west

8. What airport is just outside Washington, D.C.? _____

Reading Street Maps

A street map shows the streets and avenues in a city. It also shows where to find important places in a city.

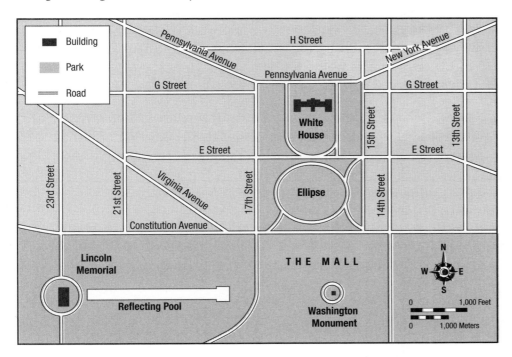

Look at this street map of Washington, D.C. Then answer the questions below.

9. Find Pennsylvania Avenue. What famous home does it go past?

_____

10. What monument is east of the Lincoln Memorial and south of the White House?

_____

11. Where is the Reflecting Pool?

Ⓐ next to the White House

Ⓑ between the White House and the Washington Monument

Ⓒ east of the Lincoln Memorial

Ⓓ east of the Ellipse

12. About how long is the Reflecting Pool?

_____

13. Imagine you just visited the Washington Monument. You are now headed to the White House along 17th Street. What should you do when you get to E Street?

Ⓐ turn right

Ⓑ turn left

Ⓒ turn around and go back to Constitution Avenue

Ⓓ nothing, since you are at the White House

LESSON 23   K-W-L: Forming Study Questions

One way to understand more of what you read in a textbook is to use the K-W-L strategy. This strategy can help you set a purpose for reading and keep track of what you learn. Here is what the letters K-W-L stand for:

- **K**now—what you **know** about the topic you are going to read about
- **W**ant—what you **want** to know about the topic
- **L**earn—what you **learn** while reading about the topic

Before Reading—Identify the Topic

You may not realize it, but when you read, you use a lot of information that you already know. That is why it helps to think about a topic before you begin reading. Look briefly at the passage on the next page.

1. What is the topic of this passage? _____

2. What did you use to figure this out? _____

What You Know and What You Want to Know

Now ask yourself what you know about the topic. Here, you might ask, "What do I already know about the first automobiles?" To keep track of your thoughts, you can begin to fill in a K-W-L chart.

3–4. Look at the chart below. List two things you know about the topic under the heading **What I Know**. (See the example in the first column.)

What I Know	What I Want to Know	What I Learn
Automobiles need fuel, such as gasoline.	When was the first car made?	

There are many things you do not know about the first automobiles. The next step before reading is to think about what you want to know.

5–6. List two questions you think of under **What I Want to Know**. (See the example in the second column.)

> **STRATEGY TIP**
>
> Turning the title and headings of a passage into questions and trying to answer them before you read is a quick way to figure out what you know about a topic.

Read the Passage

You have thought about what you know and what you want to know. Now it's time to read! As you read, look for the answers to your questions.

The First Automobiles

Key Terms

automobiles
inventors
popular
batteries
gasoline
industry

People often think cars were invented in the late 1800s. In fact, engines on wheels have been around for nearly 3,000 years.

Steam-Powered Vehicles. Writings from ancient China tell about a cart powered by steam. It was in use about 800 B.C. Much later, in about 1670, a European priest in China built a cart that used steam. In 1769 the French military built a cart for pulling guns. It also ran on steam power. That cart reached a speed of 2.5 miles per hour. But then it turned over and crashed. By 1804 British and American inventors had built passenger cars powered by steam. These quickly became popular. However, there were problems with steam engines. They were smoky and noisy. They frightened horses. Sometimes they exploded.

Electric and Gasoline-Powered Cars. From 1891 to 1905, electric cars became popular. Compared to steam cars, they were quiet and easy to use. Electric cars had problems though. They lacked speed and power. Most went no faster than 20 miles per hour. The batteries needed recharging every 50 miles.

In 1885 two Germans, Karl Benz and Gottlieb Daimler, built the first practical cars powered by gasoline. U.S. inventors quickly picked up on the idea. By the early 1900s, America had become the hub of the car industry.

In 1777, a test run of a steam carriage in Paris may have ended in the first auto accident.

After Reading—Think About What You've Learned

7–8. Look back at the K-W-L chart on page 86. Which of your questions in the second column can you answer now? If you can answer a question, write your answer in the **What I Learn** column. If you can't, write a question mark.

Here is an example K-W-L chart with the columns filled in. Notice that two of the questions in the second column couldn't be answered.

What I Know	What I Want to Know	What I Learn
Cars need fuel, such as gasoline.	When was the first car made?	The Chinese made a steam-powered cart in 800 B.C.
The first car probably was made of metal or wood.	What fuel was used in the first car?	The first cars were powered by steam. Later, they used electric power.
The first car probably was not fast.		
The first car probably could not go very far before needing more fuel.	How much did the first car cost to make?	?
	How fast could the first car go?	?
The ride was loud and bumpy.	When did cars start to use gasoline?	A gas-powered car was built in 1885.

9. What can you do if you don't find an answer to a question while reading?

Ⓐ Read the passage again to see if you missed the answer.

Ⓑ Look up information on the topic in another book.

Ⓒ Ask friends, teachers, or family members if they know the answer.

Ⓓ all of the above

When you read a passage, you will also learn things that you didn't have questions about. Should you ignore that information? Of course not! Look for main ideas and details throughout the passage. Then add this information in the **What I Learn** column under the answers to your questions.

LESSON 24   Recognizing Text Structure

Another strategy that can help you understand textbook information is to look at how the information is organized. Here are some ways information in a textbook paragraph can be organized:

- by a main idea and details
- by a sequence of events or steps

In order to see a text's structure, look for the important ideas and figure out how they are related to each other.

KEY WORDS

Main idea
the most important idea in a paragraph or passage

Detail
a small piece of information that tells more about the main idea

READING TIP

The main idea is often the first or the last sentence in a paragraph.

Main Idea and Details

Many paragraphs are organized by a main idea and details.

- The **main idea** is the most important idea in a paragraph or passage.
- **Details** are smaller bits of information that tell more about the main idea.

Read this introductory paragraph. Look for the main idea. Then answer the question below.

Assembling an Automobile

To make a car, thousands of parts must be put together. Most cars are built on a main assembly line. In an assembly line, workers do certain jobs in a certain order. At each point on the assembly line, workers attach, tighten, inspect, or test parts as they are added to the car. Then the car moves on to the next point so that something else can be done. Each part of a car must be put in place. It must fit precisely. In the early 1900s, workers attached each part by hand. Today, computers direct robots to do some of the work. Even with the robots' help, completing all of the steps takes about two days.

Key Terms

assembly line
inspect
computer
robots

---

1. Which sentence tells what the paragraph is mostly about?

   Ⓐ To make an automobile, thousands of parts must be assembled.

   Ⓑ Each part must be put in place and fit precisely.

   Ⓒ In the early 1900s, workers attached each part by hand.

   Ⓓ Even with the robots' help, completing all of the steps takes about two days.

Making an Outline

An outline can help you understand and remember the main ideas and details in a paragraph. An outline lists details under the main ideas they support.

> **Example**
>
> I. Main Idea
>   A. Detail
>   B. Detail
>   C. Detail

2–4. Shown below is the beginning of an outline for the paragraph on page 89. Read the outline. Then write other details from the paragraph in the blanks.

Main Idea: I. Thousands of parts need to be put together to make an automobile.

Details: A. Cars are put together on an assembly line.

                                1. In an assembly line, workers do certain jobs in a certain order.

                                2. _____

                                3. _____

                B. The assembly line process has changed over time.

                                1. In the early 1900s, workers attached each part by hand.

                                2. _____

Sequence of Events or Steps

Many paragraphs are organized by a sequence of events or steps.

- Sequence is the order in which events happen or the order of steps in a process.
- Sequence words such as **first, next,** and **last** help show the order.

The next paragraph tells how a car is put together. As you read it, look for the order in which the steps are done.

From the Body to the Trim. A car is put together in steps. First, the body parts are brought together. Computers direct robots to weld the body panels in place. Next, special cameras and lasers scan all of the body parts to make sure they fit together properly. Then it's time for the paint job. The car is dipped into a tank of primer, a base coat that helps prevent rust. Top coats of paint are then sprayed onto the body. The next step is attaching the body to the frame of the car. The frame includes the wheels, axles, brakes, steering column, drive train, and engine. The frame has been put together on its own assembly line. Once the body has been attached to the chassis, the windows, seats, mirrors, door handles, trim, and many other parts are added. At last, the car is ready to be driven off the assembly line.

KEY WORD

Flow chart
a chart that shows the order of steps in a process or the order in which events happen

Making a Flow Chart

A **flow chart** shows the steps in a process or the order in which events happen. A flow chart is made up of boxes and arrows.

Example

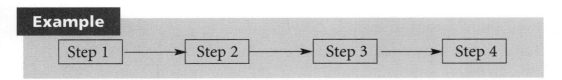

STRATEGY TIP

Sequence words such as **first, next, then,** and **finally** are clues that a passage tells the steps in a process or the order of events. Words such as **because** and **as a result** show that cause-effect relationships are being described.

5–7. The flow chart below sums up the process of putting together a car. Read the flow chart. Then complete it with information from the paragraph above.

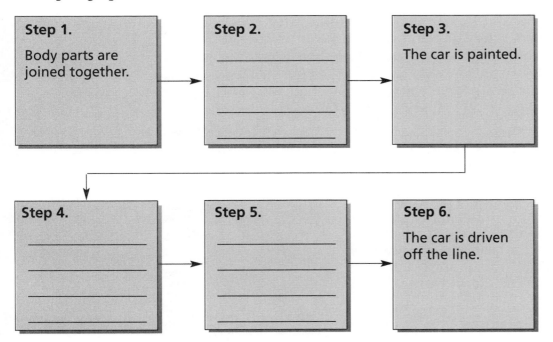

Step 1. Body parts are joined together.

Step 2. _____

Step 3. The car is painted.

Step 4. _____

Step 5. _____

Step 6. The car is driven off the line.

Part A

Previewing and Predicting

Preview the passage in the box below. (Don't read it yet.) Then answer the questions.

1. Based on your preview, what do you think this passage is about?

_____

2. How did you decide this?

_____

3. If the topic of this passage is new to you, what should you do? Circle the strategy that can help you.

skip the hard parts   read faster   read more slowly

Ocean Navigation

Using Landmarks. To navigate means to plan and control where you sail a ship. The first sailors stayed close to shore. They sailed only during the day. They used landmarks to help them know where they were. To sail at night and to travel farther out to sea, they needed another way to navigate. So they began to use the stars to help them stay on course.

Using a Compass and Sextant. After 1100 A.D., two new tools came into use. The compass has a magnetic needle that always points north. This helped sailors know which direction they were heading. The sextant allowed sailors to measure the angle from the earth to a star. Using several stars and some math, they could figure out where they were. This method did not work in cloudy or foggy weather, however.

Using a Radio and Satellite. Radio signals first came into use in 1896. Radio signals can travel through clouds and fog. In the 1940s, ships began using radar. They bounced radio signals off objects to locate them. Today, radio signals are bounced off satellites in orbit around the earth. This type of navigation system is called a global positioning system, or GPS. It has been in place since 1994. Using a GPS computer, ships can learn their exact position. They can use this system at any time, anywhere in the world, whatever the weather.

Sailors can use compasses, sextants, or GPS computers to help them find their way at sea.

Key Terms

navigate/navigation
compass
sextant
radar
satellite
global positioning
   system (GPS)

---

4. Before you read this passage, think about what you know about the topic. Fill in the first column of the K-W-L chart below. Then think about what you want to learn and fill in the second column.

What I Know	What I Want to Know	What I Learn
_____	_____	_____
_____	_____	_____
_____	_____	_____
_____	_____	_____
_____	_____	_____
_____	_____	_____

5. Now read the passage. When you have finished, complete the last column of the K-W-L chart.

Recognizing Text Structure

Part B

Read the passage on page 92 again. Then answer the questions.

1. How is the passage about ocean navigation organized? Circle your answer.

by a main idea and details   by a sequence of steps

by a sequence of events

TEST TIP

When you are asked a question about sequence, it can be helpful to create a brief list of events or steps in a process.

2. In the space below, make an outline of the first two paragraphs of the passage.

Ocean Navigation

    I. _____

        A. _____

        B. _____

   II. _____

        A. _____

        B. _____

Part C   Interpreting Graphic Aids

Look at the time line. Then answer the questions below.

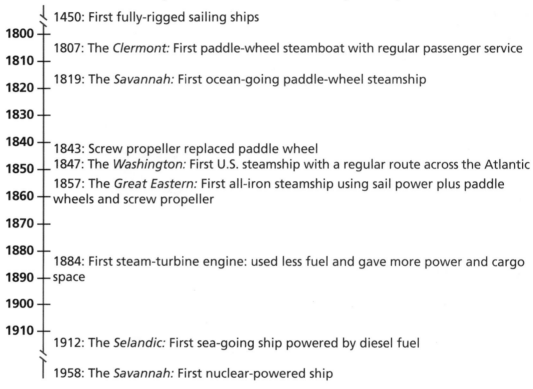

Important Firsts in the History of Ships

1450: First fully-rigged sailing ships

1800

1807: The *Clermont:* First paddle-wheel steamboat with regular passenger service

1810

1819: The *Savannah:* First ocean-going paddle-wheel steamship

1820

1830

1840

1843: Screw propeller replaced paddle wheel

1850 — 1847: The *Washington:* First U.S. steamship with a regular route across the Atlantic

1857: The *Great Eastern:* First all-iron steamship using sail power plus paddle

1860 wheels and screw propeller

1870

1880

1884: First steam-turbine engine: used less fuel and gave more power and cargo

1890 space

1900

1910

1912: The *Selandic:* First sea-going ship powered by diesel fuel

1958: The *Savannah:* First nuclear-powered ship

1. What is the topic of this time line?

_____

2. About how many years does the time line cover?
   Ⓐ 50   Ⓒ 5,000
   Ⓑ 500   Ⓓ 1,000

3. What year did the screw propeller replace the paddle wheel?
   Ⓐ 1807   Ⓒ 1847
   Ⓑ 1884   Ⓓ 1843

Complete each sentence with the correct year.

4. The first ocean-going steamship sailed in _____.

5. The first steamship to have a regular route across the Atlantic sailed in
   _____.

Reading Maps

Part D

Look at the map of the San Francisco Bay area. Then answer the questions below.

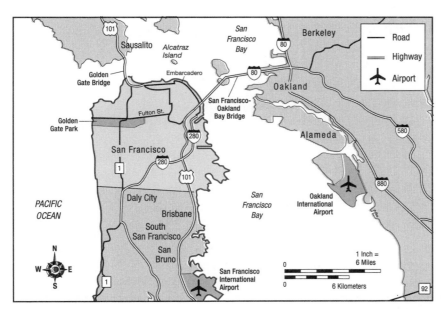

1. What direction would a ship sail when entering the San Francisco Bay from the Pacific Ocean?

   Ⓐ north

   Ⓑ south

   Ⓒ east

   Ⓓ west

2. What highway runs through Golden Gate Park?

   Ⓐ 1

   Ⓑ 280

   Ⓒ 80

   Ⓓ 880

3. Which of these cities is **not** along the path from San Francisco to the San Francisco International Airport?

   Ⓐ South San Francisco

   Ⓑ Brisbane

   Ⓒ San Bruno

   Ⓓ Oakland

4. What bridge would you cross to get from Sausalito to San Francisco?

   Ⓐ Golden Gate Bridge

   Ⓑ San Francisco-Oakland Bay Bridge

   Ⓒ Crossing a bridge is not necessary.

LESSON 25   Using Strategies to Read a Science Textbook

Science textbooks explain things in the natural world. Each chapter or section gives information about a certain topic. The information is often presented in several ways—in paragraphs, photographs, captions, diagrams, and charts.

In the last chapter you learned several strategies for reading history and geography textbooks. These can help you read and understand science textbooks too.

- Preview the text by looking at the **chapter title** and the **headings** at the beginning of each section.
- Study the information presented in **photographs**, **diagrams**, and **charts**. Read their **captions**.
- Take **notes** about what you read.
- Think about how the **text** is **organized**.
- Look for **key terms** and figure out their meanings.

In this chapter you will learn other strategies that will also be useful when you read science textbooks.

The SQRR Strategy

One way to get the most out of the books you read for your science class is to use the SQRR strategy. This strategy can help you understand even the most complex science topics.

The letters in SQRR stand for

- **S**urvey—Preview a text to see what it is about. Look quickly at the headings, the photographs and captions, and any other graphic aids.
- **Q**uestion—Turn each heading into a question or questions.
- **R**ead—Read to find the answer to each of your questions.
- **R**ecite—Explain what you have learned in your own words.

Survey and Question

To survey or preview a text, look at the title and the headings. Also look at any graphic aids, such as photographs, diagrams, or charts. Think about what the text might be telling about. Then turn each heading into a question or questions.

Survey the sections of a chapter from a science text on the next page. (Don't read it yet.)

STRATEGY TIP

If a passage does not contain the answer to a question you have posed when using the SQRR strategy, you can think of a question the passage **does** answer and use it to fill in your SQRR chart.

Volcanoes

How a Volcano Forms. The earth's crust is a layer of rock 5 to 25 miles thick. Below the crust is a ball of very hot, melted rock, called **magma**. The magma is so hot that it can melt the solid rock above it. When the solid rock melts, gases are created that then mix with the magma. These gases push the magma upward through weak places in the crust. Sometimes the magma collects in pockets. Other times it blasts through the surface. When this happens, the magma becomes **lava**, which piles up and forms a volcano.

Where Volcanoes Form. The theory of **plate tectonics** helps to explain where volcanoes form. In some places where two **plates**, or sections of the earth's crust, meet, one plate is forced below the surface. As the rock moves downward, it is melted by friction and heat from the earth's **core**. The magma may then move to the surface to form a volcano.

Volcanoes are also found in areas where two plates are moving away from each other. This occurs on the ocean floor. As the plates move apart, magma breaks through the surface. The lava piles up to create underwater mountains. Sometimes these mountains rise above the surface of the water to form volcanic islands.

1. Read these questions about the chapter sections above. Write **1** next to the question you would ask before reading the first section. Write **2** next to the question you would ask before reading the second section.

_____ **A** Where is the biggest volcano?_____ **C** Who studies volcanoes?

_____ **B** How does a volcano form? _____ **D** Where do volcanoes form?

Read and Recite

You can use a chart like the one below to keep track of what you read. The heading of each section goes in the **Survey** column. The questions you make from the headings go in the **Question** column.

Now read the passage about volcanoes. As you read, look for an answer to each of the questions in the chart. When you have finished reading, think about what you have learned.

2–3. In your own words, write what you have learned in the **Read and Recite** column.

Survey	Question	Read and Recite
How a Volcano Forms	How does a volcano form?	_____
		_____
		_____
Where Volcanoes Form	Where do volcanoes form?	_____
		_____
		_____

Apply SQRR

Use the SQRR strategy to read the next two sections of the chapter about volcanoes. Remember to survey these sections before you read.

4–5. What question would you ask yourself about each section? Write these questions in the chart below.

Now read each section.

6–7. Write your answers in the **Read and Recite** column.

Types of Volcanoes. There are several types of volcanoes. A volcano's type is based on its shape and how it was formed. A volcano called a cinder cone is created when dust, ash, and larger rocks blast out of an opening. When they fall back to earth, they may form a cone-shaped mountain. A shield volcano is formed when lava flows from an opening and spreads out. This creates a low, dome-shaped mountain. A composite volcano is formed when an eruption includes lava, dust, ash, and rocks that pile up in layers. This makes a tall, cone-shaped mountain. Some volcanoes are a combination of these types.

Effects of Volcanic Eruptions. Volcanic eruptions range in size from small to very, very large. Eruptions of any size have the power to destroy. Just one medium-sized blast can shoot out several thousand cubic feet of ash and rock. Such a blast can knock down forests and choke rivers. It can wipe out wildlife in its path. The largest eruptions create clouds of ash. These can change weather over a whole continent. Lava from larger eruptions has covered cities, destroying homes and taking lives.

Survey	Question	Read and Recite
Types of Volcanoes		
Effects of Volcanic Eruptions		

LESSON 26   Interpreting Charts, Tables, and Diagrams

Information in science books is often presented in graphic aids. There are many different types of graphic aids: pictures with captions, maps, graphs, charts, tables, and diagrams. These can help you see and compare the special characteristics of things.

- A **chart** presents information by putting facts in categories.
- A **table** presents information in rows and columns.
- A **diagram** is a drawing of a thing or a process that includes labels. The labels identify the parts of what is being shown.

Reading Charts

First, read the title and column headings of a chart. The title names the topic of the chart. The headings tell you how the chart is organized. Once you understand how the chart is organized, read the information.

Read the chart. Then answer the questions below.

Materials Blasted Out of a Volcano

Dust	Ash	Bombs and Blocks	Gas
Volcanic dust can be carried by winds all around the earth. It can change weather patterns. The dust can cause red sunsets for months or even years.	Hot ash falls to the ground and sticks together to form rock. Sometimes it mixes with water in a stream or river and becomes a hot mudflow.	Large round pieces of volcanic rock are called bombs. They can be as small as baseballs or as large as refrigerators. Huge pieces of volcanic rock are called blocks.	Gas is formed when rock melts inside the earth. The gas builds up pressure beneath the rock. When the volcano erupts, it explodes into the air.

1. Which materials get blasted out of a volcano? Fill in the correct circles.

   Ⓐ ash   Ⓒ dust

   Ⓑ clay   Ⓓ gas

2. How does ash become a hot mudflow?

   Ⓐ It turns into liquid as it cools.

   Ⓑ It passes through steam before it hits the ground.

   Ⓒ It mixes with the water in a stream or river.

   Ⓓ It creates clouds that drop muddy rain.

KEY WORDS

Chart
a table, graph, or diagram created to provide information quickly

Table
information presented in rows and columns

Diagram
a drawing of a thing or process that includes labels identifying the parts of what is being shown

Reading Tables

Tables use columns and rows to organize information. The information often includes numbers. When you come across a table, read the title first. Then read the headings of the columns and rows. Once you understand how the table is organized, you can read it to find specific information.

Read the table. Then answer the questions below.

Major Eruptions of Some Famous Volcanoes

Name	Place	Elevation, in Feet (meters)	Date of Major Eruption	Size of Eruption, in Cubic Kilometers of Ash
El Chichón	Mexico	3,478 (1,060)	1982	1
Krakatau	Indonesia	2,668 (813)	1883	18
Mount Katmai	Alaska (U.S.)	6,714 (2,047)	1912	30
Mount Mazama (Crater Lake)	Oregon (U.S.)	8,106 (2,471)	4857 B.C. (approximate)	50
Mount Pinatubo	Philippines	5,248 (1,600)	1991	2–4
Mount St. Helens	Washington (U.S.)	8,363 (2,549)	1980	1
Mount Tambora	Indonesia	9,348 (2,850)	1815	150
Mount Vesuvius	Italy	4,200 (1,281)	A.D. 79	4

READING TIP

The abbreviation B.C. stands for **before Christ**. This abbreviation follows the number for a year occurring before the birth of Jesus. For example, 500 B.C. occurred 500 years before the year in which Jesus was born. The abbreviation A.D. stands for **anno Domini,** a Latin expression meaning "in the year of our Lord." This abbreviation is used before or after the number of a year occurring after the birth of Jesus. For example, 1500 A.D. occurred 1500 years after the year Jesus was born. This date can also be written A.D. **1500,** or just **1500.**

3. What is the topic of this table?

Ⓐ the most active volcanoes in the United States

Ⓑ the oldest known volcanic eruptions

Ⓒ the tallest active volcanoes in the world

Ⓓ the major eruptions of some famous volcanoes

4. What is the elevation listed for Mount Katmai?

Ⓐ 2,047 feet   Ⓒ 6,714 feet

Ⓑ 2,667 feet   Ⓓ 8,364 feet

5. Which of these volcanoes had a major eruption most recently?

Ⓐ Mount Pinatubo   Ⓒ Mount St. Helens

Ⓑ Mount Vesuvius   Ⓓ Mount Mazama

6. How many years passed between the major eruptions listed for Krakatau and Mount Tambora?

Ⓐ 10   Ⓒ 68

Ⓑ 37   Ⓓ 92

Reading Diagrams

Science information can also be presented in a diagram. A diagram is a drawing with labels or captions. It shows a process or the parts of something. When you study a diagram, read the title, look at the picture, and read the labels or captions. Pay careful attention to lines or arrows that connect the written information to parts of the picture.

Study this diagram of an erupting volcano. Then answer the questions below.

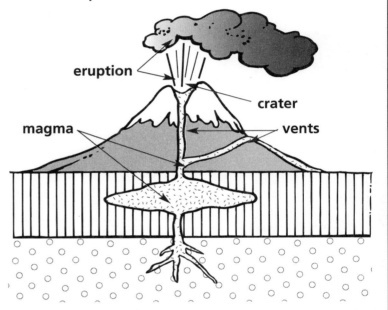

How a Volcano Erupts

magma Hot magma flows upward from deep inside the earth toward its crust. It pushes into cracks and pockets in the crust. It is so hot that it melts the solid rock above it.

vent Magma forces its way up to the surface. It travels through a tall vent or chimney. Sometimes a side vent forms off the main vent.

eruption The flow of magma blasts out of the vent into the air. Steam, ash, and gas form a huge cloud. Red-hot lava spills out at the top and flows downhill.

crater After a volcano erupts, some of the flow sinks back into the vent. This forms a dish or bowl-shaped crater.

7. What does magma travel through just before reaching the surface?

    Ⓐ a vent or chimney   Ⓒ a crater

    Ⓑ a pocket   Ⓓ a cloud

8. Where does a crater form?

    Ⓐ inside a pocket of magma

    Ⓑ beneath a vent or chimney

    Ⓒ above a cloud of ash

    Ⓓ at the spot where a volcano erupts

LESSON 27   Taking Notes

When you read a science textbook, it's important to keep track of the information presented. Maybe you will be writing a report about a science topic. Maybe you are going to be tested on the material. Either way, it's a good idea to take notes as you read. Notes can help you understand what you read. They can also help you study for tests and quizzes.

Here are some tips for taking notes:

- **Rewrite the information** in your own words. Use key phrases that will help you remember the information. Keep your notes short, so they will be easy to review.
- **Organize your notes** the way the text is organized. Here are some methods to try:
  - Use a bulleted list or an outline to show main ideas and details.
  - Use a numbered list to show a sequence of events or steps.
  - Use a flow chart to show a process.
  - Use a sketch or diagram to show the parts of an object.

Notes About Insects

Read the passage below. Then read the notes on the card on page 103 that one student took.

Insects, Insects Everywhere. Insects—small creatures with six legs—are the world's largest group of animals. They make up about two-thirds of all animal species that have been discovered. Insects are found almost everywhere in the world. They live on mountaintops and in deserts. They are found under the ground and in the sky.

Friends or Enemies. Different kinds of insects have different relationships with other living things. Some insects are helpful. They pollinate plants. They make things people use, such as silk and honey. They help keep the earth clean by eating the remains of dead plants and animals. They serve as food for other animals.

Insects can also be harmful. Some sting and are poisonous. Some carry diseases, such as malaria and bubonic plague. Others cause huge problems for crops. Grasshoppers sometimes eat whole fields of corn plants. Aphids drink sap from pea plants, causing them to shrivel and die. Many other kinds of insects are plant pests too. Potato beetles, caterpillars, leaf hoppers, stalk borers, whiteflies, moths, and tomato hornworms are just a few of the insect enemies farmers must battle.

Insects
- Insects are everywhere.
  - large part of animal kingdom
  - live all over the world
- Insects can be good.
  - pollinate plants
  - make things people use (honey, silk)
  - keep environment clean
- Insects can be bad.
  - carry diseases
  - harm crops
    - eat plants (grasshoppers)
    - drink sap (aphids)

1. How are the notes on this card organized?

    Ⓐ a bulleted list or an outline   Ⓒ a flow chart

    Ⓑ a numbered list   Ⓓ a sketch or a diagram

2–4. Read the information below. Draw a line from each detail on the left to the main idea on the right.

Insects are the world's largest group of animals.

    • Insects can be bad.

Insects eat the remains of dead plants and animals.

    • Insects can be good.

Some insects sting and are poisonous.

    • Insects are everywhere.

5. Which of these details could you add to the notes under **Insects can be good**?

    Ⓐ have six legs   Ⓒ serve as food for other animals

    Ⓑ make up about two-thirds of all animal species   Ⓓ cause problems for farmers

More Insect Notes

Now read this passage about insects.

Controlling Insect Pests. People have found many ways to control insect pests. Farmers often change the crops they grow. This keeps insects that eat one crop but not another from multiplying year after year. Farmers also plant crops at times of the year when some pests are not as common.

Insecticides. Many farmers and gardeners protect their plants by using insecticides. These are poisons sprayed over a field or garden to kill insect pests. Using insecticides has its own dangers, however. These poisons can kill helpful insects, such as butterflies. The poisons can get into the plants and animals that people eat. Also, some pests get used to the poisons over time. When that happens, the poisons don't kill them anymore.

Insects to the Rescue. Using insects to fight insects is usually less harmful than using poisons. Many insects have insect enemies. For example, ladybugs eat insect eggs, aphids, and mites. One tiny wasp attacks moth eggs before they hatch. The tachinid fly hunts caterpillars and other bugs. The praying mantis eats grasshoppers, aphids, and stalk borers. These insects help control insect pests in ways that are not harmful to plants, animals, or people.

6–13. Review the passage. Then complete the notes on the card.

Controlling Insect Pests
- Change crops or planting times
- Use insecticides
  - what they are: _____
  - how they are used: _____
  - some dangers/problems
    - _____
    - _____
    - _____
- _____
  - many insect pests have natural insect enemies
  - what they do: _____
  - examples: _____
  - benefit: control pests without harming plants, animals, people

LESSON 28   Skimming and Scanning

Most science books contain information about many different topics. Sometimes you may be looking for specific information about a topic. Or you may have a question or questions that you want to answer. Skimming and scanning are two strategies you can use to find the information you want in a science book.

- When you **skim** a text, you look it over quickly to figure out the topic.
- When you **scan** a text, you look for key words or terms to help you find specific information you are looking for.

KEY WORDS

Skim
to look over text quickly to figure out the topic

Scan
to look for key words or terms to help you find specific information

Skimming

To skim a science chapter, read the title. Then read the headings and the first sentence of each paragraph. Also, look at pictures and other graphic aids and read any captions.

Try skimming this passage. (Don't read it yet!) Then answer the first question on page 106.

Solar-Powered Vehicles

Powered by Sunlight. Solar-powered vehicles, or SPVs, use solar cells for power. These cells use sunlight to make electricity. People have made cars, planes, boats, and even bicycles that run on sunlight. SPVs have large solar panels, called arrays, made of many solar cells. The panels are placed in a way that allows them to catch as much sunlight as possible. The fastest sun-powered cars can go more than 80 miles per hour! Most travel at about 40 miles per hour.

Solar-powered cars can store electricity in a battery to use when the sunlight is not strong.

1. Based on your skimming, which question do you think this passage will answer?

   Ⓐ Why is the sun so bright and hot?

   Ⓑ How do solar-powered vehicles (SPVs) use sunlight?

   Ⓒ Why are sport utility vehicles (SUVs) popular?

   Ⓓ Where are solar cells made?

2. Now read the passage. Did it answer the question you chose? If so, write the answer below. If not, go back and choose a different question. Then write the answer.

   _____

   _____

   _____

Scanning

Often you must look for specific information in a science book. To find that information, you can scan the section it's likely to be in. First, ask this question: What do I want to know? Next, look quickly through the text to find key words related to what you want to know. Then read the sentences containing the key words to find the information you are looking for.

Suppose you want to know how solar energy gets from a solar cell to a battery. Quickly scan the passage below to find the information. (Hint: Look for the word *battery*.)

> **How a Solar Cell Works.** A solar cell is made of thin layers of a material such as silicon. One layer has more than the normal number of electrons. The other layer has fewer than normal. When sunlight shines on the solar cell, electrons flow from one layer to the other. If a wire is attached to the layers, the electrons will flow through it. This forms an electric current. The current flows from the wires into a battery or motor.

3. How does solar energy get from a solar cell to a battery?

   _____

   _____

   _____

Apply Skimming and Scanning

Skim the following passage to learn what it is about.

> **Safe and Clean.** Solar energy is a safe, clean source of power. Using sunlight for power does not cause smog or acid rain. Also, solar energy does not use up our limited supply of fossil fuels. There is plenty of sunlight for all. Solar energy is not widely used, however. The equipment needed to make it is expensive. This makes solar power more costly than power obtained by burning fossil fuels.

4. What is the topic of this passage? _____

_____

_____

Now think of something you'd like to find out about the topic. Write a question about this below. Then scan the passage to find the answer.

5. Question I want to answer: _____

_____

_____

_____

6. The answer: _____

_____

_____

_____

LESSON 29   Organizing Information Graphically

KEY WORDS

Compare and contrast
to tell how two things
are alike and how they
are different

Cause and effect
a reason for an event or
condition, and a result of
the event or condition

In the last chapter you learned some ways information in history and geography textbooks is organized:

- by a main idea and details
- by a sequence of events or steps

These methods of organization are used in science textbooks too. In addition, science textbooks often organize information by comparing and contrasting. When textbooks **compare and contrast,** they tell how two things are alike and how they are different. Textbook information may also be organized by **causes and effects**. This method explains the reason for something as well as the result, or effect, of it. This lesson will give you practice reading text organized by comparisons and contrasts and by causes and effects.

Recognizing Causes and Effects

Read the passage below. As you do, pay attention to the series of events that cause a rocket to be pushed upward.

> **Rocket Engines.** For their size, rocket engines are the most powerful of all engines. The power produced by a rocket is about 3,000 times as great as the power produced by a car engine of the same size.
>
> **How a Rocket Engine Makes a Rocket Fly.** A rocket engine works by burning fuel very fast. As the fuel burns, it produces hot gases. These gases expand quickly. They push against the inside walls of the rocket. The gases also rush out the open end of the rocket with great force. The rocket begins to move upward. It goes faster and faster as more fuel is burned.

1. What is the structure of this passage?

   Ⓐ It compares and contrasts two things.

   Ⓑ It states a main idea and gives supporting details.

   Ⓒ It explains a series of causes and their effects.

   Ⓓ It states an opinion and gives supporting facts.

THINK ABOUT IT

Some causes can have more than one effect, and some effects can have more than one cause. Can you think of any examples? Some events can be both a cause **and** an effect. Ask yourself: Did event A happen because of event B, or the other way around?

Cause-and-Effect Chart

The graphic organizer below is a cause-and-effect chart. You can use a chart like this to keep track of causes and effects described in a science book.

2–3. Read the information in the chart. The column on the left tells whether an event is a **cause** of another event, an **effect** of another event, or both. Fill in the blank parts of the chart.

cause	Fuel inside rocket engine burns.
effect/cause	
effect/cause	Gases push against sides of rocket and out opening against ground.
effect	

WRITING TIP

You can organize your own writing using cause-and-effect relationships. You might use a cause-and-effect chart to organize your ideas before writing.

Recognizing Comparisons and Contrasts

Sometimes in science texts, two inventions, processes, or creatures are described together. Thinking about how the two things are alike and how they are different can help you better understand them.

Read the passage. Then answer the question below.

Types of Rocket Engines

Every rocket has a chamber in which fuel is burned. As the fuel burns, it creates gases. These provide the thrust that lifts the rocket. The opening the gases travel out of is called the nozzle.

Solid-Fuel Rockets. Solid-fuel rockets burn a rubber-like solid fuel. A small amount of black powder is burned to ignite the fuel. Once the fuel starts to burn, it cannot be stopped easily. It burns until it is gone. However, the solid fuel is easy to store for long periods of time. Also, it is generally not dangerous unless ignited. Solid-fuel rockets are used to launch spacecraft. They are also used in fireworks displays.

Liquid-Fuel Rockets. Liquid-fuel rockets burn various types of liquid fuel. The fuel is usually ignited by some sort of spark. This type of rocket is easier to stop and start. The fuel supply can be shut off by closing the valve to the fuel tank. Liquid fuel creates more force when it burns. It generally explodes more easily than solid fuel, though, so it is more dangerous to store and handle. Liquid-fuel rockets are used to move spacecraft around once they are in space.

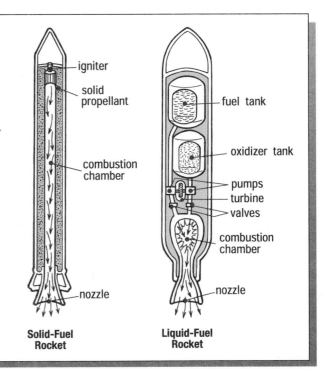

Solid-Fuel Rocket: igniter, solid propellant, combustion chamber, nozzle

Liquid-Fuel Rocket: fuel tank, oxidizer tank, pumps, turbine, valves, combustion chamber, nozzle

4. How are the paragraphs in this passage organized?

Ⓐ by listing the steps in a process

Ⓑ by comparing and contrasting two things

Ⓒ by explaining causes and effects

Ⓓ by giving an opinion and listing facts that support it

Venn Diagram

You can use a Venn diagram to organize the information in a passage that compares and contrasts two things.

5–9. Fill in the missing parts of this Venn diagram with information from the passage on page 109.

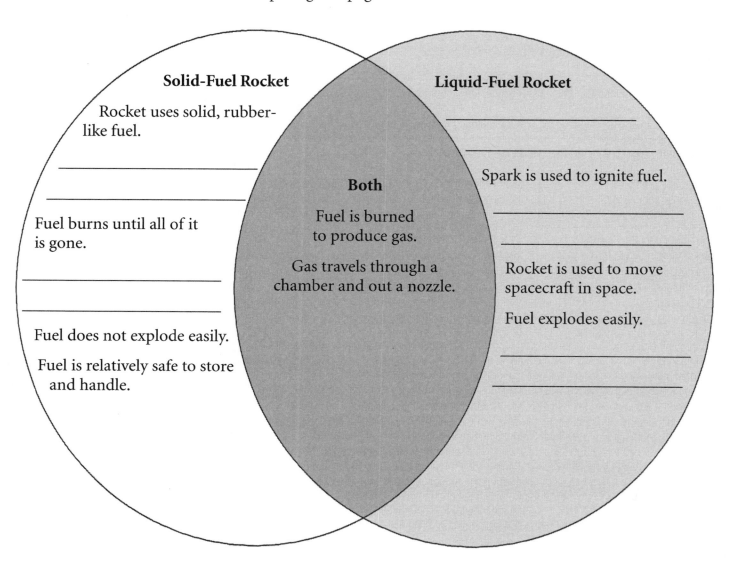

Solid-Fuel Rocket

Rocket uses solid, rubber-like fuel.

_____

_____

Fuel burns until all of it is gone.

_____

_____

Fuel does not explode easily.

Fuel is relatively safe to store and handle.

Both

Fuel is burned to produce gas.

Gas travels through a chamber and out a nozzle.

Liquid-Fuel Rocket

_____

_____

Spark is used to ignite fuel.

_____

_____

Rocket is used to move spacecraft in space.

Fuel explodes easily.

_____

_____

LESSON 30   Understanding Technical Terms

Each field of science has a special set of words to name and describe things. Science books often include key term lists and glossaries to help readers learn the meanings of these terms. Knowing how to use these features will help you better understand what you read. Using word parts, context, or a dictionary will also help you figure out the meanings of key terms.

Using a Key Term List and a Glossary

Many science books list key terms at the beginning of each chapter. These are important words and phrases that may not be familiar to you and other readers. If definitions are given, be sure to read them. If definitions are not given and the book has a glossary, look up each term to find its meaning.

Breaking Words into Parts

As you read passages in science books, you will come across unfamiliar words that are not listed as key terms or defined in the glossary. One good way to figure out the meaning of an unfamiliar word is to break it into smaller parts. Then you can look for parts you know. If you understand one or more parts of a word, you may be able to figure out its meaning.

Read the following sentence:

> The hydrosphere includes all oceans, lakes, and rivers, as well as ice, snow, clouds, fog, and mist.

Use what you know about the word parts *hydro* and *sphere* to figure out the meaning of *hydrosphere*. Complete the sentence below.

1. The hydrosphere is the part of the earth that is made up of _____.

Ⓐ rock   Ⓒ water

Ⓑ air   Ⓓ fire

Now read this sentence:

> Some oceanographers are trying to understand how sound travels through water.

2. Fill in the circles next to the word parts in **oceanographers** that could help a reader figure out its meaning.

Ⓐ ocean   Ⓒ ogre

Ⓑ graph   Ⓓ er

The words around an unfamiliar word can help you figure out its meaning. To give you an example, read this sentence: "As Rick hiked across the glacier, he narrowly missed falling into a crevasse." The words **glacier** and **falling into** are clues to the meaning of **crevasse**: "a huge, deep hole in ice or snow."

Think about the meanings of these word parts to figure out the meaning of *oceanographers*. Then fill in the correct circle below.

3. Oceanographers are _____.

Ⓐ people who study and write about oceans

Ⓑ people who live near oceans

Ⓒ graphs about oceans

Ⓓ ogres that live in oceans

Using Definitions That Appear in Text

Sometimes the author of a science book will define a key term within the context of a sentence or a paragraph. Often, that definition appears between commas right after the word.

Read the following sentence. Then fill in the correct circle.

Geomorphologists, people who study how the earth's surface has changed, discovered that the island was a dormant volcano.

4. A geomorphologist is someone who_____.

Ⓐ studies the sky and stars

Ⓑ solves geometry problems

Ⓒ studies how the earth's surface has changed

Ⓓ knows how to change volcanoes into islands

Thinking of Related Terms

You can figure out the meanings of some unfamiliar words by thinking of related forms of these words. For example, you might not know the meaning of the word **equatorial,** but if you know the related word **equator,** you may be able to figure out the meaning of the new word: "near the equator."

Using a Dictionary

In Chapter 1 of this book, you practiced using a dictionary. Take a moment to review how to use a dictionary:

- Look at the beginning letters of the word you are looking up.
- Look at the guide words at the top of a page. Find two that have the same beginning letters your word has. Figure out whether your word comes between these words.
- Look through the entry words to find your word.
- Read the definitions and find the one that matches how the word is used in the text you are reading.

Use a dictionary to find the definitions of the terms in bold type. Write each definition on the line.

5. The **seismogram** showed that a minor earthquake had occurred.

_____

6. The **friable** rock eroded very quickly.

_____

7. The hikers found large amounts of **obsidian** near the volcano crater.

_____

STRATEGY TIP

You can use more than one strategy to figure out a word meaning. For example, you can look up a word in the dictionary. Then you can use context clues to figure out which of the dictionary meanings fits the way your word is used in its sentence.

Applying the Strategies

Read the paragraph. Then answer the questions.

Tracking Earth's Changes by Satellites

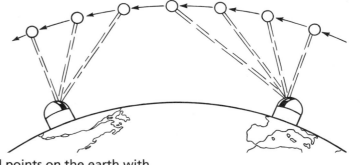

Geodesy is the science of making precise measurements of the earth. **Geodetic satellites** keep track of changes in the earth's surface. The **LAGEOS** is one of these satellites. It looks like a giant ball covered with mirrors. The term **LAGEOS** comes from the words laser, **geo**dynamics, and satellite. Its mirrors reflect pulsed **lasers**. They send these light beams back to stations on the ground.

Scientists measure how long it takes for the lasers to bounce back to the earth. In this way, they can determine the **ranges,** or distances, between widespread points on the earth with great precision. Even very slight changes in the earth's surface can be tracked. This is called **satellite laser ranging,** or **SLR**.

8. What is a **laser**? _____

What strategy or strategies did you use to figure out this word?

Ⓐ used word parts   Ⓒ from related words

Ⓑ from sentence context   Ⓓ used a dictionary

Ⓔ other: _____

9. What does **range** mean in this passage? _____

How did you figure out this word? Check all the strategies you used.

Ⓐ by using word parts   Ⓒ from related words

Ⓑ from sentence context   Ⓓ by using a dictionary

Ⓔ other: _____

Part A   Using the SQRR Strategy

Use the SQRR strategy with the text and chart below.

1–2. First, survey the text. Figure out the questions you want to answer and write them in the **Question** column of the chart.

3–4. Next, read the text and write your answers in the **Read and Recite** column. Then add anything else you learned.

Space Stations

Skylab. In 1973 the United States launched its first space station. The station, called Skylab, had two solar panels to provide electricity for the machines on board. One panel was damaged during the launch from Earth. Less than two weeks later, three astronauts arrived. They fixed the solar panel and made other repairs. They stayed on board Skylab for 28 days. Within the next year, two other crews worked on Skylab. One stayed in space for 59 days and the other for 84 days. They carried out experiments, made space walks, observed the sun, and took pictures of Earth.

The International Space Station. After Skylab, the United States planned a larger, more lasting space station. By 1993 it had become an international project. Sixteen countries now share in the building and operation of the new International Space Station, or ISS. Construction began in 1998, with a planned completion date of 2004. The ISS will be the biggest space station ever. Each piece is built on the ground and attached in space. The first crews came aboard in 2000. Space crews live aboard the ISS for more than 100 days at a time. They conduct research and go on space walks while maintaining the space station.

Survey	Question	Read and Recite
Skylab	_____ _____ _____ _____	_____ _____ _____ _____
The International Space Station	_____ _____ _____ _____	_____ _____ _____ _____

Look at the space station diagrams. Then answer the questions below.

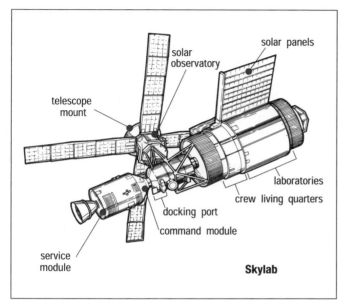

Skylab

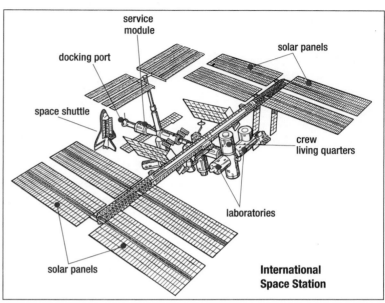

International Space Station

5. Which feature is shown on the ISS, but not on Skylab?

Ⓐ laboratories

Ⓑ a space shuttle

Ⓒ solar panels

Ⓓ crew living quarters

6. Where did spaceships attach to Skylab?

Ⓐ at the crew living quarters

Ⓑ at the solar panels

Ⓒ at the docking port

Ⓓ at the telescope mount

THINK ABOUT IT

What information can a diagram show that text by itself cannot? How are these diagrams like photographs? How are they different?

Organizing Information Graphically

Part B

Reread the passage on space stations and answer the questions.

1. How are these paragraphs organized?

Ⓐ by a sequence of events

Ⓒ by causes and effects

Ⓑ by a main idea and details

Ⓓ by an opinion and facts that support it

2. On a separate sheet of paper, take notes about the passage on page 114. Your notes should show how the information is organized. For example, you might use a chart, an outline, or a Venn diagram.

Part C

Skimming and Scanning

Skim the following passage. (Don't read it yet.)

Life in Space

Search for Extra-Terrestrial Intelligence (SETI). People often wonder whether there is life in outer space. Some scientists think life could exist on other planets. They have been looking for signs of life in space for more than 40 years.

SETI Projects. Many SETI projects are going on right now. Most use **radio telescopes** to gather signals from space. One project uses the world's largest radio telescope to look at faraway stars. This telescope is in Arecibo, Puerto Rico. Another project uses a big radio telescope to scan the whole sky. Still another project uses **optical telescopes**—telescopes for the eye. With these, scientists look for short laser bursts from stars.

1. What is this passage about? _____

Now scan the passage to find the answer to this question:

2. What is special about Arecibo, Puerto Rico? _____

_____

Read the passage above.

3. Use this notecard to take notes about the passage.

Life in Space

_____

_____

_____

_____

_____

_____

_____

_____

Understanding Technical Terms

Part D

Look at the passage about life in space on page 116. Answer the questions.

1. What is the meaning of the word **faraway** in the second paragraph?

_____

How did you figure out the meaning of this term? Fill in the circle next to each strategy you used.

Ⓐ word parts

Ⓒ related words

Ⓑ a definition presented in context

Ⓓ a dictionary

Ⓔ other: _____

2. What does **optical** mean? _____

_____

What strategy or strategies did you use to figure out the meaning of this term?

Ⓐ word parts

Ⓒ related words

Ⓑ a definition presented in context

Ⓓ a dictionary

Ⓔ other: _____

3. What is a **radio telescope**? _____

_____

What strategy or strategies did you use to figure out the meaning of this term?

Ⓐ word parts

Ⓒ related words

Ⓑ a definition presented in context

Ⓓ a dictionary

Ⓔ other: _____

LESSON 31   Reading the Newspaper

Daily
a newspaper that is printed every day

Weekly
a newspaper that is printed once a week

Knowing how to read a newspaper is an important skill for staying informed. Most newspapers are either **dailies** (printed every day) or **weeklies** (printed once a week). Each issue of a daily paper has news articles about important local, national, and international events. It also tells about local events.

Parts of a Newspaper

The articles in a newspaper are organized in sections. The main sections usually include the Front Page section, Local News, Business, Sports, and The Arts. There may also be sections about food, travel, or technology. The descriptions below tell you what is in each section.

Front Page
This section presents the most important news from the previous day. The stories focus on local, national, or international events. They cover a wide variety of subject areas.

Business
This section gives news about the world of business. Stories may focus on industries, companies, business people, or financial markets. The classified advertising pages (also known as want ads) in this section list jobs that are available.

The Arts
This section lists local art and cultural events, including museum displays and concerts. It also gives movie reviews and TV listings.

Local News
Sometimes local news is given its own section. It is usually called the Metro, Regional, or Local News section. This part of the paper tells about events, politics, jobs, and important people in your city or area. It also has a page with persuasive essays called editorials. These give the newspaper's opinions on topics. The editorial page also includes persuasive essays from outside writers (op-ed pieces) and letters to the editor from readers.

Sports
News and scores from the sports world are given in this section. Usually several stories about local teams are printed each day. Stories and scores for national and international sports leagues are also included.

Use what you know about the parts of a newspaper to answer these questions. Fill in the correct circle.

1. In which part of the newspaper would you look to find the score of a baseball game?

   Ⓐ Sports   Ⓒ The Arts

   Ⓑ Business   Ⓓ Metro

2. In which section would you expect to find an essay giving an opinion about an upcoming election?

   Ⓐ Front Page   Ⓒ Metro

   Ⓑ Business   Ⓓ Sports

3. Where would you look to find jobs that are being advertised?

   Ⓐ Sports   Ⓒ The Arts

   Ⓑ Business   Ⓓ Metro

4. Where could you find out what time a new TV show is on?

   Ⓐ Front Page   Ⓒ Sports

   Ⓑ Business   Ⓓ The Arts

Parts of a Newspaper Article

Most news stories have the same main parts. Read the labels below to learn the purpose of each part.

A **headline** is printed above a story in large type. It briefly tells what the story is about.

A **dateline** tells where and when the story was written.

The **lead** is the first paragraph of the story. It briefly and clearly states what the story is about.

President to Visit Downtown Today

Important state tour to end at City Hall.

by Manny Arroyo

BIG CITY, IA, April 12 — President Abe Smith will wrap up his tour of the state today with a public speech in front of City Hall at 2:00 p.m.

The President has spent the last two weeks traveling throughout Iowa. He has met with Governor Johnson as well as Senator Garret.

A **subhead** is printed below a headline. It gives an important detail about the story.

A **byline** gives the name of the reporter who wrote the story.

The **body** of the story is the part of the article after the lead. It gives more details about the topic described in the lead.

KEY WORDS

Headline
words in bold type that briefly tell what a story is about

Dateline
a line that tells where and when a story was written

Lead
the first paragraph of a news story

Subhead
words printed below the headline that give an important detail about the story

Byline
a line that gives the name of the reporter who wrote a story

Body
the part of a news story after the lead

Use the news story at the right to complete items 5 to 10.

5. Write the story's headline here:

_____

_____

6. Underline the story's subhead.

7. Who wrote the story?

_____

8. When was the story written?

_____

9. Put a star next to the story's lead.

10. What is this story about? _____

_____

Tigers Beat Bears in Double OT

Carter's shot sends team to second round of playoffs.

by Ben Tomason

SKYTOWN, TX, May 1 — Mike Carter banked in a 10-foot jumper at the end of the second overtime to lead the Tigers to a 110-109 win over the visiting New York Bears last night.

Carter's shot fell with only 0.3 seconds remaining, and the Bears were unable to get off another shot as time expired. The victory vaults the Tigers into first place.

Newspaper index
a listing that shows where to find specific information within a newspaper

Classified advertisement
a description of an item for sale, a listing of a job that is open, or an offering of a service

STRATEGY TIP

When you pick up a newspaper that is new to you, looking at the index is often the fastest way to find the section or feature you are looking for.

HELP WANTED

PAINTERS WANTED P/T. $200/wk. No exp req. Can't fear heights. 763-555-1212

TYPIST NEEDED F/T. No exp but 60 wpm req. $30K/yr. 763-555-7711

FOR RENT

1 BR apt in new building. $900/mo. No fees. 763-555-1117

FOR SALE

1991 Ford. 200K miles. Good cond. $2100 or b/o. 763-555-6583

Newspaper Index

To find specific information in a newspaper, you can use the **newspaper index**. It is usually found at the bottom of the front page of the paper. Each section of the paper is given a different letter. The index lists each section with its letter and page number.

Read the newspaper index at the right. Then use it to answer the questions.

11. On what page would you find tomorrow's weather forecast? _____

12. What would you find on page D8?

_____

13. On what page might you find a review of the latest movie?_____

14. On which pages would you find local news? _____

Index

Box Scores E1
Business News C1
Classified Ads C7–15
Comics D8
Editorials B13
Local News B1–5
Movie Reviews D6
Puzzles D9
Weather B12
World News A1–4

Classified Advertising

Classified advertisements in a newspaper list items people want to sell. They also include job listings and business services. The lists are arranged by category. Each ad is printed in small type with abbreviations. Here are some abbreviations used in classified advertising.

P/T	= part-time	yr	= year	b/o	= best offer	wpm	= words per
F/T	= full-time	exp	= experience	apt	= apartment		minute
wk	= week	K	= 1,000	BR	= bedroom	cond	= condition
mo	= month	req	= required				

Read the classified ads at the left. Then use them to answer the questions.

15. What is one job being advertised? _____

16. How much does this job pay? _____

17. How many bedrooms are there in the apartment for rent?_____

18. What is the price of the car that's for sale? _____

LESSON 32   Thinking Critically About the News

Different types of writing in a newspaper have different purposes:

- A news article's purpose is to inform readers about a current event.
- An editorial's purpose is to present an opinion about a topic. Its writer tries to persuade others to feel similarly or to act in a way that goes along with that opinion.
- An advertisement's purpose is to persuade readers to purchase a particular product or service.

Knowing the purpose of a piece of writing can help you read it critically. It can help you decide if the writer has done a good job of presenting facts, expressing an opinion, or persuading others.

Thinking Critically About News Articles

Newspaper reporters are supposed to be objective. They are supposed to present the facts of an event fairly, without including their own feelings or opinions. However, reporters do not always succeed in being objective. Readers should ask themselves questions to decide whether an article is fair.

Editorial
a short persuasive essay

Appeal
an ad that tells what a product is or how it works

Testimonial
an ad in which someone supports a product

Product comparison
an ad that compares a product with other brands and points out why one is better

Read the following information from witnesses and the beginning of an article. Think critically about the information presented in the article. Then answer the questions.

Witness A: Sailboat Captain
"I sent a radio message saying I was ready to go under the bridge. Then I started sailing. I've done this a million times. He just waited too long to raise the bridge!"

Witness B: Bridge Operator
"He never said he was sailing under the bridge. All I heard was, 'Get the bridge up quick!' I did my best, but it was already too late. He forgot to send me a radio message."

Witness C: Man Walking By
"The boat smashed right into the bridge. Cars couldn't cross for hours. People were yelling and screaming. What a mess!"

Bridge Accident Stops Traffic

BAY CITY, CA, July 2 —A sailboat crashed into an unopened drawbridge at 2:00 p.m. yesterday. As a result, downtown traffic was stopped for several hours.

The accident happened when the boat's captain failed to radio the bridge operator.

"All I heard was, 'Get the bridge up quick!'" said the operator. "I did my best. But it was already too late."

1. Which witness does the reporter seem to use as the main source for what happened?

   (A) witness A   (C) witness C

   (B) witness B   (D) no sources were used

2. Who does the news reporter seem to blame for the accident?

   (A) the man walking by   (C) the sailboat captain

   (B) the bridge operator   (D) nearby drivers

3. Does the article present facts about whether the sailboat captain sent a radio message to the bridge operator? ___ yes ___ no

4. Do you think the news article presents the facts fairly? Why or why not?

   _____

   _____

Thinking Critically About Editorial Opinions

One place where newspaper writers are allowed to give opinions is the editorial page. **Editorials** are short persuasive essays. They give the writer's opinion on a topic or issue. Editorials talk about many subjects, including local, national, and international news and politics. Newspapers also use the editorial page to support political candidates before elections.

When you read an editorial, notice the reasons the writer gives to support his or her opinion. Ask yourself: Are they convincing?

Read the editorial at the right. Then answer the questions.

5. The writer's opinion is that the mayor _____.

   Ⓐ should cut firefighters' pay

   Ⓑ should give himself a raise

   Ⓒ should get rid of violent crime

   Ⓓ should increase police pay

6. What is one reason the writer gives to support his opinion?

   _____

7. Do you think the writer's argument is convincing? Why or

   why not? _____

   _____

Thinking Critically About Advertisements

Almost half the space in the average newspaper is filled with advertising. Ad writers do not need to be objective. They use many methods to try to sell products or services. Being able to understand and recognize these methods is an important skill for buying wisely. Here are some commonly used advertising methods.

- **Appeals** are ads that tell what a product is or how it works. They also try to show you how the product will make your life better if you buy it.
- **Testimonials** are ads in which someone supports a product. Many of these ads use famous people, such as athletes or actors.
- **Product comparisons** are ads that compare a product with other brands and point out why one is better than the others.

Look at the ad at the right. Answer the questions below.

8. What kind of ad is this?

   Ⓐ appeal   Ⓒ product comparison

   Ⓑ testimonial

9. What is one opinion in this ad? _____

10. Does this ad make you want to buy Shine-O car wax? Why or why not?

   _____

   _____

THINK ABOUT IT

Based on the limited information in the editorial above, do you agree with the writer's opinion about a pay raise for the police? Why or why not?

SHINE-O Car Wax

Shine-O Car Wax will make your car look faster. You'll be the coolest person on your block.

Get a Can Today!

LESSON 33 Reading and Following Instructions

KEY WORD

Instructions
written steps that tell
you how to make or
do something

Instructions are written steps that tell you how to make or do something. They can be anything from a recipe for chocolate chip cookies to directions for putting together a lawn mower. Being able to read and follow directions is another important real-life reading skill.

Here are some tips for reading and following directions.

- Read all the way through the instructions. Make sure you understand each step before beginning to do the work.
- Most instructions include a list of materials needed. Read the list and make sure you have all necessary parts and tools before you begin.
- The steps in instructions are written in the order in which they should be done. Numbered lists or sequence words, such as **first, then,** and **finally,** help you know what to do first, next, and so on.
- Some instructions include diagrams showing where parts are located or how they fit together. These will help you understand the instructions.

Following Assembly Instructions

Read the instructions below.

How to Attach a Bike Rack

Parts and Tools
- 4 strut bars
- 4 small C clamps
- 10 bolts
- 2 mounting bars
- 1 rack platform
- 1 small wrench

Steps
1. First, bolt the ends of two strut bars to form a V-shaped strut arm. Then do this for the other two strut bars.
2. Next, bolt the two loose ends of each strut arm to the sides of the rack platform.
3. Lower the rack body over the rear tire, so the rack platform is directly behind the seat.
4. Bolt the corner of each strut arm to the brazon near the rear wheel axle. (*Brazons* are holes built into bikes for attaching racks.)
5. Next, bolt the two mounting bars to the brazons under the bike seat.
6. Adjust the bolts to fit securely.

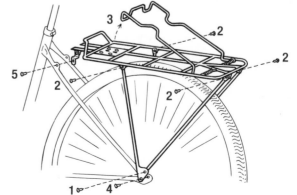

Now answer these questions.

1. Put these steps in the correct sequence by numbering them 1 to 4.

_____ **A** Adjust the bolts and clamps to fit securely.

_____ **B** Bolt the two mounting bars to the brazons under the bike seat.

_____ **C** Lower the rack body over the rear tire.

_____ **D** Bolt the ends of two strut bars to form a V-shaped strut arm.

2. Which of these parts is **not** listed in the instructions?

Ⓐ strut bars

Ⓒ bolts

Ⓑ tire pump

Ⓓ rack platform

3. Circle the part of the diagram that shows where to attach the mounting bars to the brazons under the bike seat.

4. Put a box around the part of the diagram that shows where to bolt the corner of each strut arm to the brazon near the rear wheel axle.

Following Game Instructions

Now read this set of instructions.

How to Play Bocce

Bocce can be played anywhere—on grass, dirt, or sand, on level ground or a hill.

Equipment
- 8 large bocce balls (4 of one color, 4 of another color). Balls may be made of wood or metal. They must be of equal size.
- 1 small target ball called a **pallino**. The pallino must be a different color than the bocce balls.

Playing the Game
1. A coin is tossed. The team that wins gets to toss the pallino.
2. A member of the team that won the coin toss rolls the pallino onto the playing field. He or she may roll the pallino in any direction, as far as he or she chooses.
3. The "nearest ball" rule controls the order of thrown balls. The player who tossed the pallino rolls his or her first bocce ball toward the pallino. That player then steps aside and doesn't bowl again until the other team has gotten one of its balls to stop closer to the pallino.
4. The side whose ball stops closest to the pallino is called "in," and the other team is called "out." Whenever a team gets "in," it steps aside and lets the "out" team bowl. This goes on until both sides have used all their balls.
5. A player may also try to use a ball to "spock" (knock away) any of the other team's balls in play.

Scoring
1. When all balls have been thrown, the two teams measure the distance of the balls from the pallino.
2. Teams earn 1 point for each ball that is closer to the pallino than the nearest ball of the other team.
3. In case of a tie between two balls of opposing teams, the balls can cancel each other's score or may be played again by the same players.

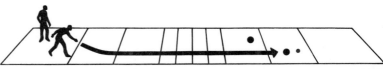

Use the game instructions on the previous page to answer these questions.

5. How many balls do you need to play this game?

(A) 8

(C) 2

(B) 4

(D) 9

6. What is the **first** thing that happens after the coin toss?

(A) The first player steps aside and doesn't bowl again until the other team has gotten a ball closer to the pallino.

(B) A member of the team that won the coin toss rolls the pallino onto the playing field.

(C) A player spocks the other team's closest ball.

(D) A team rolls its four balls at the pallino all at once.

7. What should you do **after** your team gets "in"?

(A) Step aside and let the "out" team bowl.

(B) Toss the coin again to see who goes next.

(C) Roll the rest of your balls at the pallino.

(D) Measure the distance of your team's balls from the pallino.

8. What does it mean to "spock" a ball belonging to the other team?

_____

_____

LESSON 34   Consumer Products

Most products you buy come with written material. This material may be printed on the package. It may be printed in a separate booklet inside the package. Or it may be printed on the product itself.

The table below lists several types of products. It also tells what written information is usually included with each type.

Type of Product	Information
prepared foods	amount (weight or volume), ingredients, nutrition facts, directions for preparation (if necessary), expiration or packaging date, recipes
toys or games	instructions, list of parts, additional materials needed but sold separately (such as batteries), number of players, appropriate age levels
electronic products	instructions, specifications (size, dimensions, power requirements), list of features, safety information, warranty or registration, optional accessories, contact information (phone number, Web address)

Reading About Prepared Foods

Reading and understanding the information labels on prepared foods is very important. Making good choices about what you eat can give you the energy you need and keep you healthy. Most prepared foods have a label that lists ingredients, from the most-used ingredient to the least-used ingredient. The label also gives nutritional information:

- the size of a single serving
- the number of calories per serving
- the amount of fat, protein, and carbohydrates per serving
- the recommended daily amounts of nutrients and salt per serving

STRATEGY TIP

The labels with nutritional information follow a standard format established by the U.S. government. Becoming familiar with this format can help you find the information you need quickly.

Think About What's Inside

Read the nutrition facts from a cereal box on the next page. Then answer the questions.

Nutrition Facts

Serving Size	1 cup
Servings Per Package	About 20

Amount Per Serving	Cereal	with ½ cup Skim Milk
Calories	120	160
Calories from Fat	12	12
	% Daily Value	
Total Fat 1g	2%	2%
Saturated Fat 0g	0%	0%
Cholesterol 0mg	0%	0%
Sodium 170mg	8%	11%
Total Carbohydrate 23g	8%	10%
Dietary Fiber 1g	4%	4%
Sugars 7g		
Protein 2g		
Vitamin A	10%	15%
Vitamin C	10%	10%
Calcium	10%	20%
Iron	35%	35%

INGREDIENTS: CORN MEAL, WHOLE GRAIN OATS, SUGAR, CORN SYRUP, WHEAT STARCH, CALCIUM CARBONATE, SALT.

1. What ingredient does this cereal contain the most of? _____

2. What ingredient does it contain the least of? _____

3. What is the serving size? _____

4. How many servings does the box of cereal contain? _____

5. How many total calories are in one serving with milk? _____

6. How many of these calories are from fat? _____

Reading About Other Products

Here are some tips for using the written information that comes with other types of products.

- The information on labels can help you decide what to buy. Here is an example: You want to put a microwave oven on a countertop in your kitchen. The dimensions listed on an oven's label can help you figure out if it will fit.
- User manuals and instruction sheets tell you how to use products properly.
- Warranty cards should be filled out and sent back to the manufacturer. If you send in the card, the manufacturer will fix or replace the product you bought if there's a problem when you first use it.

Look for Useful Information

Read the film package label at the left. Then answer the questions.

Colorific
35mm Color Negative Film
for Photographic Prints with Rich, True Colors
2-Pack

Colorific
2-Pack
400 ASA
Process C-41
Daylight Balanced
36 Exposures per Roll x 2 Rolls

7. What company makes this film?

ⓐ American Standards Association (ASA)

ⓑ Colorific

ⓒ Photographic Prints, Inc.

8. What kind of camera does this film work in?

ⓐ advanced photo system (APS) camera

ⓑ digital camera

ⓒ 35mm camera

9. What kind of pictures can you take with this film?

ⓐ black-and-white prints

ⓑ slides

ⓒ color prints

10. How many pictures can you get from this pack?

ⓐ 2

ⓑ 36

ⓒ 72

Imagine that you want to use this film with a new camera. You have some questions, so you get out the instruction manual that comes with the camera. You turn to the table of contents, which looks like this:

**Snapco 35mm Point-and-Shoot Camera
Instruction Manual**

Now answer these questions.

11. Is the film shown on the opposite page the correct type for your Snapco camera? Explain. _____

_____

12. What page in the manual gives instructions for loading film? _____

13. Imagine that you've loaded the film properly. You've also followed the directions for taking pictures. The film won't advance, however. On what page in the manual should you look for help? _____

14. What page will tell you if you can buy a carrying case made for your camera? _____

Comparing Two Products

Read the product labels for two pogo sticks at the right. Then answer the questions.

15. Which pogo stick would be better for an adult? Why?

_____

_____

16. If you want a pogo stick that won't break, which of these should you buy? Why?

_____

_____

Kangaroo Jumper
Heavy-Duty Pogo Stick
$70
- Air shock absorber for smooth ride
- Chrome finish
- Limited 3-year warranty

Warning: Excessive pogo stick jumping can cause headaches.

Hopper's Pogo Stick $45
★ Super coiled spring action
★ Lifetime Warranty
(You'll never have to buy another pogo stick!)
★ Oldest pogo stick company in the country

Warning: Not suitable for children over 90 lb.

LESSON 35   On the Job

KEY WORD

Company handbook
a book that describes the
rules of a company

If you work or have worked, then you know that reading is a part of almost any job. Some jobs, such as teaching, publishing, and acting, involve a lot of reading. Others jobs involve less. However, no matter what you do, your job will require some reading. After all, right at the beginning you have to read to fill out a job application. Most jobs also have forms you must use, such as time sheets, contracts, and tax forms.

Reading Company Handbooks

Many businesses issue a **company handbook** or manual. The handbook usually lists company rules and procedures. It also gives other official policies, safety information, and phone numbers within the company. Below is a sample page from the employee handbook at Rudy's Record Shop.

Store Opening

The store will open promptly at 10 a.m. every day of the week. If you are scheduled to open the store, you must obtain the store keys from a manager on your previous shift. (If you lose the keys, you must pay a $10 replacement charge.) Arrive at 9:45 a.m. and follow these steps:

- Enter the store and turn off the alarm. To turn off the alarm, press #7839 (#-R-U-D-Y) on the alarm keypad. Lock the door once you are inside.
- Turn on all the store lights and the copy machine in the office.
- Check the answering machine for messages and the fax machine for faxes.
- Turn on the cash register and fill the register tray with the proper bills and coins from the safe (see Register Procedures on page 10).
- Once these steps are complete, unlock the front door.

CD Pricing

If you are asked to price CDs, follow these guidelines:

- New CDs are always $16.95 unless they appear on the discount list in the office.
- Once a CD has been out for four months, the price goes down to $14.95. Check the catalog in the office for release dates.
- Import CDs are usually $21.95, but check with a manager before pricing imports.
- CD singles are normally $7.95.
- Some specialty items may have higher or lower prices. Check with a store manager if you are unsure.

3

STUDY TIP

If you are given a copy of a company manual to keep, read all of it as soon as you can. You may want to underline or highlight rules and procedures that are important to the job you do.

Use the Handbook

Answer these questions. Use the information in the employee handbook you just read.

1. When do employees opening the store get the keys to the store?

   Ⓐ when they are first hired

   Ⓑ on the morning they are to open the store

   Ⓒ during the last shift the day before they will open

2. Which of these duties must be done when opening the store? Fill in the circle next to all that apply.

   Ⓐ turn on the cash register

   Ⓑ turn on all the lights and the copy machine

   Ⓒ turn off the alarm

   Ⓓ sweep the store

3. How can an employee tell if a CD is considered a new release?

   Ⓐ by looking at the year of the copyright on the CD itself

   Ⓑ by waiting four months and then asking a store manager

   Ⓒ by checking a catalog in the office

4. What should an employee do if he or she is not sure of the price for an import CD?

   Ⓐ call another store to see what they are charging

   Ⓑ take it to a cashier and see how much he or she charges

   Ⓒ ask a store manager for help

   Ⓓ look up the price on the Internet

Reading Company Directories

Many businesses include a listing of company phone numbers in their handbook. Others print the numbers in a separate list. You will need to know how to read a company **phone directory** for most jobs.

Keep in mind these tips when using a company phone directory:

- The direct numbers, known as **extensions,** may be four digits or less.
- The entries may or may not be in alphabetical order.
- Look for instructions that tell you how to dial an outside number, how to transfer calls, how to put someone on hold, and how to answer other lines when they ring.

KEY WORDS

Phone directory
a book or list of names and telephone numbers

Extension
an extra telephone connected to the main line

Use a Directory

Read the following example of a company phone directory.

Phone Directory

To get an outside line, dial 9. To dial an extension from an outside phone, add the 555 prefix to the four-digit extension number (for example, the main number is 555-7839, or 555-RUDY). To transfer a call, press the transfer button, dial the extension number, and then press #.

Main Number 7839
Pop Department 7840
Classical Department 7841
Jazz Department 7842
Used CD Buyer 7843
Accounting 7844
Security 7845
Fax Machine 7846

In case of emergency, dial 9, then 911.

Answer these questions.

5. What is the extension number for Security? _____

6. What number would you dial to reach the Jazz Department from an outside phone?_____

7. What would you do to transfer a call to the Classical Department?

_____

8. What should you dial in case of emergency?_____

LESSON 36   Internet Safety

The Internet is a useful tool. It can help you find information on almost any subject. However, you must be careful. Otherwise you may give other people personal information you don't want them to have. Remember these tips:

- Don't give out personal information unless you are certain of who is collecting the information and why they are doing it. Personal information includes your name, address, Social Security number, and credit card information.
- Internet purchases should always be made over a secure connection. This means the information is scrambled so that no one can intercept it and use it. Most Web browsers can be set to tell you when you enter a secure Web site.
- Be aware of who has access to your e-mail address. The more you give out your e-mail address, the more likely it will be added to junk mail or "spam" lists.

- Don't give out passwords (such as your e-mail password), even if you are asked to while online. Company representatives should not ask you for this information. When in doubt, e-mail the customer service department of the company. Ask about their policy.
- If you use the Internet to do real-time "chat," use caution. Don't give out any personal information to strangers. It is probably best to keep Internet friendships on the Internet. Above all, don't be pressured into meeting a stranger in person.

Safety Check

Read the following situations and answer the questions.

1. You want to buy a book from a Web site. Now it's time to enter your personal information and credit card number. Your computer is set to notify you when you enter a secure site or a site that is not secure. A window pops up to tell you that this site is not secure. There is a link on the page for a secure version of the page. What should you do?

   Ⓐ Enter the information asked for and press Submit.

   Ⓑ Go to the secure page. Then enter your information there.

   Ⓒ Set your browser so it doesn't notify you when a site is not secure. Try again.

If you are using the Internet to do research for a report, try to figure out the reliability of each of the sources you plan to use. Governmental (.gov) and educational (.edu) sites are likely to contain accurate information. For other sites, be sure to identify who the source is and what type of expertise or experience he or she has on the subject.

2. You are surfing the Web when a window pops up. It says, "This is your Internet service provider. Please confirm your e-mail address and password in order to stay online. We are checking to make sure only authorized users are accessing our service." What should you do?

Ⓐ Type in your e-mail address and password immediately.

Ⓑ Type in the credit card number you used to open the account.

Ⓒ Ignore the message. Check with your service provider to see if this is really the policy.

3. You have been e-mailing and chatting online with a new "electronic pen pal." You are getting along very well, and now your new friend would like to meet in person. What should you do?

Ⓐ Meet at your new friend's house.

Ⓑ Meet at a popular hamburger place near your house.

Ⓒ Tell your friend you are happy with the friendship just the way it is.

Quality Check

Almost anyone can put information on the Web. How can you tell the good information from the bad? Here are some questions to ask yourself:

- **Who is providing the information, and why?** A source such as an educational Web site is more likely to provide unbiased information than is a company that is trying to sell you something.
- **Is the information paid advertising?** It's not always easy to tell whether something you see is an advertisement in disguise. If a Web article only praises one product or company, it may be a message created to convince you to buy something.
- **Does the information fit with what you know?** If the information in a Web article seems strange, check it against other sources.
- **How old is the information?** A Web site may tell you how recently it was updated. If it doesn't, you can try the links on it to see how many work. A Web site with many discontinued links may be out of date.
- **Is the information presented well?** Are there a lot of misspellings on a Web site? If so, the information itself may also contain mistakes. However, remember that looks can be deceiving. Just because a site looks professional doesn't mean it's unbiased. Read critically.

Evaluating Sources

Read this article taken from the Internet. Then answer the questions.

4. What is the purpose of this article?

   Ⓐ provide information

   Ⓑ state an opinion

   Ⓒ sell a product

5. Fill in the circle next to the best choice. This source seems_____.

   Ⓐ unreliable

   Ⓑ somewhat reliable

   Ⓒ very reliable

   Explain your answer. _____

   _____

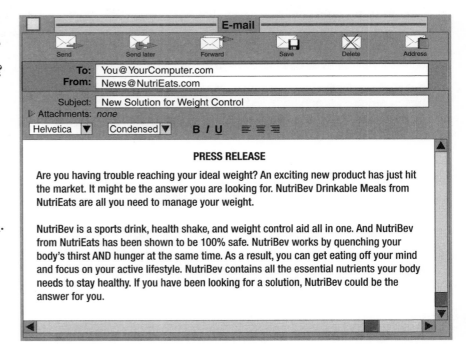

PRESS RELEASE

Are you having trouble reaching your ideal weight? An exciting new product has just hit the market. It might be the answer you are looking for. NutriBev Drinkable Meals from NutriEats are all you need to manage your weight.

NutriBev is a sports drink, health shake, and weight control aid all in one. And NutriBev from NutriEats has been shown to be 100% safe. NutriBev works by quenching your body's thirst AND hunger at the same time. As a result, you can get eating off your mind and focus on your active lifestyle. NutriBev contains all the essential nutrients your body needs to stay healthy. If you have been looking for a solution, NutriBev could be the answer for you.

Now read this article from the Internet. Answer the questions.

6. What is the purpose of this article?

   Ⓐ provide information

   Ⓑ state an opinion

   Ⓒ sell a product

7. Fill in the circle next to the best choice. This source seems_____.

   Ⓐ unreliable

   Ⓑ somewhat reliable

   Ⓒ very reliable

   Explain your answer. _____

   _____

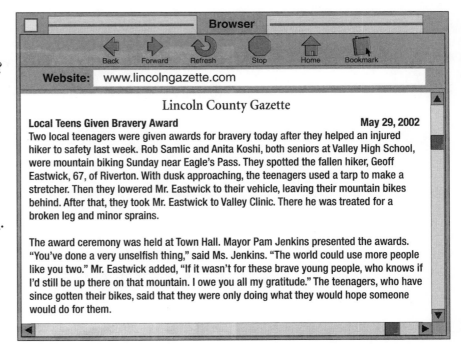

Lincoln County Gazette

Local Teens Given Bravery Award   **May 29, 2002**

Two local teenagers were given awards for bravery today after they helped an injured hiker to safety last week. Rob Samlic and Anita Koshi, both seniors at Valley High School, were mountain biking Sunday near Eagle's Pass. They spotted the fallen hiker, Geoff Eastwick, 67, of Riverton. With dusk approaching, the teenagers used a tarp to make a stretcher. Then they lowered Mr. Eastwick to their vehicle, leaving their mountain bikes behind. After that, they took Mr. Eastwick to Valley Clinic. There he was treated for a broken leg and minor sprains.

The award ceremony was held at Town Hall. Mayor Pam Jenkins presented the awards. "You've done a very unselfish thing," said Ms. Jenkins. "The world could use more people like you two." Mr. Eastwick added, "If it wasn't for these brave young people, who knows if I'd still be up there on that mountain. I owe you all my gratitude." The teenagers, who have since gotten their bikes, said that they were only doing what they would hope someone would do for them.

Part A

Reading and Thinking About the News

Use what you know about newspapers to answer these questions.

1. Where in the newspaper would you look to find the results of an election in France?

   Ⓐ Front Page   Ⓒ The Arts

   Ⓑ Business   Ⓓ Metro

2. Where would you look to find the date and time for a parade in your city?

   Ⓐ Front Page   Ⓒ The Arts

   Ⓑ Metro   Ⓓ Sports

READING TIP

Knowing the author's purpose for a particular piece of writing can help you read it critically.

---

3. Which questions should you ask yourself when you read a news article? (You may fill in more than one circle.)

   Ⓐ Does the article present both sides of the issue?

   Ⓑ How long is the article?

   Ⓒ Does the reporter seem to have an opinion about the issue?

   Ⓓ Does any information seem to be missing?

4. Which of these should you find in a well-written editorial? (You may fill in more than one circle.)

   Ⓐ a clearly stated opinion

   Ⓑ sensible reasons supporting the opinion

   Ⓒ funny jokes

   Ⓓ facts that go against the opinion

Reading and Following Instructions

Part B

Read the recipe. Then answer the questions below.

Fruit Smoothie Recipe

Ingredients:

1 ripe banana

1 cup frozen berries

1 cup milk

4 tablespoons vanilla yogurt

1/2 cup orange juice

Directions:

1. Peel the banana and break it into pieces. Place the pieces in a blender.

2. Add the other ingredients.

3. Blend for about 30 seconds.

4. Turn off the blender. Mix the smoothie with a wooden spoon.

5. Blend again for another 30 seconds.

6. Pour into tall glasses. Serve with a straw.

Makes about two 12-ounce smoothies.

---

1. Put these steps in the correct sequence by numbering them 1 to 4.

____ **A** Pour into tall glasses.

____ **B** Place the banana pieces in a blender.

____ **C** Blend for 30 seconds.

____ **D** Add the other ingredients.

2. Which of these **don't** you need to make and serve fruit smoothies?

Ⓐ blender

Ⓒ wooden spoon

Ⓑ bowl

Ⓓ tall glasses

3. How many tablespoons of yogurt do you need to make four 12-ounce smoothies?

Ⓐ 2

Ⓒ 6

Ⓑ 4

Ⓓ 8

4. Do you think this recipe needs a diagram? Why or why not?

_____

_____

TEST TIP

Pay special attention to numbers and number words in test questions. They can be tricky. For example, question 3 on this page asks how much yogurt is needed to make **four** 12-ounce smoothies. But the recipe makes **two** 12-ounce smoothies. So you can't just look at the amount in the recipe—you have to double it, because four smoothies is double the amount the recipe makes.

Part C   Consumer Products

Read the information on this product package. Then answer the questions.

1. Which of these items do you need to purchase separately in order to run the ScrubsAll?

   Ⓐ a toothbrush   Ⓒ a washcloth

   Ⓑ a comb   Ⓓ four D batteries

2. What should you do to find warranty information?

   Ⓐ look on the other side of the package

   Ⓑ look inside the package

   Ⓒ look on the company's Web site

   Ⓓ ask someone at the store

3. Should you buy this product as a gift for an 8-year-old child? Why or why not?

   _____

   _____

Internet Safety

Part D

Read this situation and answer the question.

1. You receive an e-mail from an unfamiliar source. It says that you have won a fabulous prize. To get the prize, you are asked to visit a Web site and give the following information: your name, home address, telephone number, and e-mail address. What should you do?

   Ⓐ visit the Web site and give the requested information

   Ⓑ forward the e-mail to a friend

   Ⓒ delete the message

TEST TIP

When you finish a test, take time to look it over again. Make sure you answered every question. Try it now! Look back over this practice test. Did you complete every item?

Read the sample information taken from the Internet. Then answer the question.

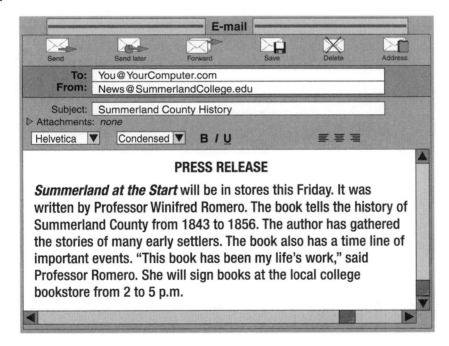

E-mail

Send   Send later   Forward   Save   Delete   Address

To: You@YourComputer.com
From: News@SummerlandCollege.edu

Subject: Summerland County History
▷ Attachments: *none*

Helvetica ▼   Condensed ▼   **B** *I* U

PRESS RELEASE

Summerland at the Start will be in stores this Friday. It was written by Professor Winifred Romero. The book tells the history of Summerland County from 1843 to 1856. The author has gathered the stories of many early settlers. The book also has a time line of important events. "This book has been my life's work," said Professor Romero. She will sign books at the local college bookstore from 2 to 5 p.m.

2. Fill in the circle next to the best choice. This source seems_____.

   Ⓐ unreliable   Ⓑ somewhat reliable   Ⓒ very reliable

   Explain your answer. _____

   _____

GLOSSARY

Abbreviation a short form of a word

Adjective a word that describes a person, place, or thing

Adverb a word that describes an action

Almanac a book of facts that is updated every year

Antonym a word that means the opposite of another word

Appeal an ad that tells what a product is or how it works

Atlas a book of maps

Bar graph a graph with bars that represent numbers

Body one or more paragraphs in a written response giving details that explain the answer; the part of a news story after the lead

Byline a line that gives the name of the reporter who wrote a story

Caption words located next to a picture that tell what the picture shows

Card catalog a manual way of organizing information about books in a library

Cause and effect a reason for an event or condition, and a result of the event or condition

CD-ROM dictionary a dictionary located on a compact disc and accessed through a computer

CD-ROM encyclopedia an encyclopedia located on a compact disc and accessed through a computer

Chart a table, graph, or diagram created to provide information quickly

Classified advertisement a description of an item for sale, a listing of a job that is open, or an offering of a service

Company handbook a book that describes the rules of a company

Compare and contrast to tell how two things are alike and how they are different

Compass rose a drawing that shows the four main directions on a map

Concluding sentence the last sentence of an ending paragraph

Consumer a person who buys goods or services

Context clue nearby words that help you figure out a word's meaning in a sentence

Copyright page a page that lists the year a book was printed, who owns the rights to the book, and the number of times the book has been printed

Daily a newspaper that is printed every day

Dateline a line that tells where and when a story was written

Definition the meaning of a word

Detail a small piece of information that tells more about the main idea

Dewey decimal system a library organizing system that puts books into categories by topic

Diagram a drawing of a thing or process that includes labels identifying the parts of what is being shown

GLOSSARY

Dictionary a book that gives information about words, including pronunciation, part of speech, other forms of the word, meanings, sample use, and history of the word

Driver's education a training class that prepares you to take a driver's license test

Editorial a short persuasive essay

Educated guessing eliminating answer choices that are clearly wrong and making the best choice from the remaining answer choices

Electronic database a large collection of online information about library resources that is organized for rapid search and retrieval

Encyclopedia a reference set that contains factual articles about many topics and is organized into volumes

Ending paragraph a last paragraph that sums up what is being said in a written response

Expository writing writing that tells about a real-life topic or explains something

Extension an extra telephone connected to the main line

Fiction stories about events that did not really happen

Flow chart a chart that shows the order of steps in a process or the order in which events happen

Focus question a question at the beginning of a chapter in a book that helps set a purpose for reading

Globe a map of the world that is in the shape of planet Earth

Glossary a list of definitions that explain important words or topics used in a book

Graphic aid something that gives information in a visual way

Guide words words at the top of a dictionary page that name the first and last entry words on that page

Heading a key word or phrase naming the topic of an article or section

Headline words in bold type that briefly tell what a story is about

Index a list of topics in a book and the page numbers where you can read about the topics

Instructions written steps that tell you how to make or do something

Key term an important word or phrase that is explained in a chapter

Latitude how far north or south of the equator a place is

Lead the first paragraph of a news story

Learner's permit a paper that states that you are learning to drive

Legend a list of symbols that stand for information on a map

Longitude how far east or west a place is from the prime meridian

Main idea the most important idea in a paragraph or passage

Map a drawing that shows the locations of places in an area

GLOSSARY

Multiple-choice question a question that gives a set of answer choices

Narrative writing writing that tells a story

Newspaper index a listing that shows where to find specific information within a newspaper

Noun a word that names a person, place, or thing

Online dictionary a dictionary located on the Internet and accessed through a Web browser on a computer

Online encyclopedia an encyclopedia located on the Internet and accessed through a Web browser on a computer

Online test a test taken on a computer

Opening paragraph a first paragraph that tells what you are writing about

Outline an organized list of main ideas and details

Periodical a publication issued on a regular schedule, such as a magazine

Phone directory a book or list of names and telephone numbers

Pie chart a pie-shaped drawing that shows the sizes of the parts that make up a whole

Predict to say what you think will happen

Preview to look ahead

Product comparison an ad that compares a product with other brands and points out why one is better

Pronunciation the way to say a word

Reference book a book with useful information that has been carefully organized

Related article another article linked to a topic

Scale of miles a drawing that shows how much an inch of space on a map stands for in miles

Scan to look for key words or terms to help you find specific information

Search engine a Web site that helps you search for information on the Internet through the use of key words

Skim to look over text quickly to figure out the topic

Subhead words printed below the headline that give an important detail about the story

Subheading a word or phrase that names one of the main ideas in an article, section, or chapter

Subtopic a smaller, more specific topic

Synonym a word that has almost the same meaning as another word

Table information presented in rows and columns

Table of contents a list of all the chapters in a book and the page number each chapter starts on

Testimonial an ad in which someone supports a product

Thesaurus a book that lists synonyms and antonyms of words

Time line a graphic aid that shows events in time order on a line

GLOSSARY

Title page the first page of a book

Topic sentence the opening sentence of a written
response to a question

Verb a word that names an action

Weekly a newspaper that is printed once a week

Writing prompt an instruction that tells you
what information to include when
answering a question with a written
response